W9-AZG-757

The Dow Jones-Irwin
Guide to
Put and Call Options

The Dow Jones-Irwin
Guide to
Put and Call Options

Henry K. Clasing, Jr.

Revised Edition

Dow Jones-Irwin Homewood, Illinois 60430

© DOW JONES-IRWIN, 1975 and 1978

All rights reserved. No part of this publication may be
reproduced, stored in a retrieval system, or transmitted,
in any form or by any means, electronic, mechanical,
photocopying, recording, or otherwise, without the prior
written permission of the publisher.

This publication is designed to provide accurate and
authoritative information in regard to the subject matter
covered. It is sold with the understanding that the
publisher is not engaged in rendering legal, accounting, or
other professional service. If legal advice or other expert
assistance is required, the services of a competent
professional person should be sought.
*From a Declaration of Principles jointly adopted by a Committee
of the American Bar Association and a Committee of Publishers.*

ISBN 0-87094-148-8
Library of Congress Catalog Card No. 77–085775
Printed in the United States of America

11 12 13 15 K 8 7 6

To My Mother and Father

Foreword to the Revised Edition

I concluded the foreword of Mr. Clasing's previous book with "I am sure we will hear further from this gifted young man." He has come forward once again.

The continuing growth in the use of options as an investment tool is ably reflected in the update of Mr. Clasing's book. The advent of puts in Chicago and other option markets is a most important development.

Mr. Clasing correctly shows the why and how of puts. Its meaning—its use—the margin—the tax implication—the strategy—all of this is added to his original book. His competence and ability to make it coherent will add to the enjoyment of the serious reader.

LEON POMERANCE
Donaldson, Lufkin & Jenrette
New York, N.Y.

Preface

A s Leon Pomerance stated so wisely in his
foreword to the first edition, this book
should be viewed as a continuing form of education. This new edition includes premium curves
for puts as well as curves to operate a neutral
hedge strategy with puts. Michael Greenbaum
of First Options of Chicago, should be thanked
for exposing me to his well-thought-out approach
to put versus call premiums. Many varieties of
spreading techniques developed since the first
edition and Humphrey Lloyd should be thanked
for his permission to use the type of spread
matrixes presented in his book, *Spread Trading
in Listed Options*. Gerald Appel deserves many
thanks for his regular inclusion of the Market
Barometer data in his excellent advisory letter,
Systems and Forecasts. He also should be given
credit for the probability tables used in the chapter on straddles.

The most important part of getting a book
into print obviously lies in preparation of a man-
uscript. In accomplishing this, Judy Hagemann
not only did an excellent job of editing, but offered a great amount of encouragement and support along the way.

December 1977   HENRY K. CLASING, JR.

Preface to the First Edition

This book was written for the serious and patient investor who is willing to devote time and energy toward achieving above-average long-term investment success. Its purpose is to explain in detail how stock options are traded. Particular emphasis is given to the structure and operation of the new options exchanges. My major theme is that trading options can be integrated into a prudent overall investment strategy.

This book differs from other books written on the subject of options in several ways. The most significant difference is the explanation of several alternative strategies based on different risk/reward objectives. I have devoted an entire chapter to those tangential aspects of investment management that often prescribe what strategy prevails: taxes and credit. A great deal of effort has been made to illustrate concepts through tables and graphs. After reading this book, the reader will have a sound set of rules to use when trading options.

The greatest amount of thanks for help in creating this book must go to Leon Pomerance. In helping to make this book a competent treatment of the subject he has given the most valuable gift anyone can offer, his precious time. Joseph Gahtan gave me the basic logic he used when quoting over-the-counter options for many years. His recommendations helped me immensely in designing the Risk Scoring Method for quoting OTC options found in the appendix. Neil Boyle must be given credit for teaching me his own special techniques for spreading which, through his combination of accounting background, trading skill, and expertise in decision making, have been developed to a fine art. Many thanks are due Jean Clasing for her many helpful comments along the way.

Producing a finished product is not an easy job, but Hildegard Vetter and Sara Cowen gave many long hours at the typewriter keyboard, helping through corrections and revisions until the job was complete. They deserve many thanks.

Contents

List of Figures

Figure

List of Tables

Introduction

1

S tock options have survived many ups and downs throughout history. The typical historical narrative mentions the origin of options as a security in relation to the tulipomania of 17th-century Holland when family fortunes were squandered speculating on the ever-rising prices of tulip bulbs. Later, they were associated with corporate raids to take over railroads in the 19th century United States or with trust building in the 1920s. They were once outlawed in England after the collapse of the South Sea Bubble and were almost prohibited in 1934 during the congressional investigations which followed the Great Crash of 1929. These were the developments that made headlines, but, behind the scenes, a small group of people known as option writers quietly made consistent profits interrupted by an occasional bear market. The important fact to remember is that despite all the controversy options survived.

Now, options have been given a new vitality. Five years ago a small number of option professionals conceived a new idea, the fungible option. If they could create an option that was standardized enough in terms of exercise prices and expiration dates and combine it with a clearing corporation which could act as guarantor, options would take on a whole new dimension. Instead of a one-on-one relationship between a buyer and seller as in the old put and call options they placed the clearing corporation in the middle to break the direct link. The result was the creation of an aftermarket for the new options which introduced tremendous flexibility in terms of the investor's ability to establish or close out his positions.

The more one understands about the structure of the new options exchanges, their ground rules for operation and the type of underlying stocks involved, the more the insight of these pioneers is appreciated. These are truly wise men. They knew the tricks and loopholes well enough to design a vehicle which is not easily tampered with. Most of the designers spent their entire careers dealing with options, and they are committed to giving the new options a long life. In the early stages, as several speculative abuses began to surface, the exchange guidelines for trading were adjusted to eliminate the problem almost as soon as it occurred. In fact, the Securities and Exchange Commission, which is normally dubious about stock brokers' willingness to police themselves, has been pleasantly surprised with the manner in which potential problems have been snuffed out by the industry leaders.

Occasionally a magazine article will call the new options exchanges a gambling casino.[1] It is

---

[1] Andrew Tobias, "Everyone's Buying Options—but does the S.E.C.?", *New York Magazine*, April 29, 1974.

hoped that the reader will find after reading this book that, in a world where nearly everything is a gamble, at least the new options offer many avenues to handle the odds and much more so than a traditional stock exchange. If a stock is purchased, there is only one direction for the price to move to realize a profit, up. Yet this book will introduce several strategies that yield a substantial profit even if a stock moves 10 percent above *or below* the price at which a stock is purchased. Even with the riskiest option strategy, buying an option, the investor can lose no more than he paid for the option, which might be several hundred dollars. But, for this he is given a reasonable chance to double or triple his money over a short period of time. Even in the best bull markets less than one stock in five doubles in two years. And if a mistake is made in buying a stock, several hundred dollars might not even cover the commissions and taxes.

To understand options one must realize that they are mainly a substitute means of dealing with the underlying stock. This means that, to be successful with options, one must also be able to successfully invest in stocks, except for one major difference. Many option strategies offer much more latitude in terms of how a profit can be made. For example, a profit can be made writing a call if the stock remains at the same price, drops in price, or rises in price less than the amount of the option premium by the end of the option's life.

Every now and then a magazine article or a book is written which tells of a fortune made with options as if it were readily available to anyone.[2] This is a cruel promise. What the author usually doesn't say is that the experience happened once, almost by accident, and hasn't happened again. When a bull market occurs and the headlines are packed with tales of fortunes being made, it is tempting to think that with a little money and a small investment of time, the reader can do the same. This is the first step towards trouble. Whether in 17-century Holland or in the United States of the late 1920s, the trouble began when people began to leave worthwhile pursuits in order to gamble their life savings on becoming rich.[3] And it wasn't just simple folk. The most intelligent, well-to-do people were duped. One of the lessons of history is that when the public begins to believe they have discovered a new way of investing to get rich quick, a certain class of scoundrel will gladly accommodate them and lose their money. In 1929, the vehicle was the leveraged investment trust. And the reason people were so financially destroyed after the Great Crash was that they borrowed even more money after the initial drop in order to recoup their losses. The steady erosion of stock prices into 1932 just finished them off.

The important lessons to learn from history are that it is consistency and good money management that counts. Bernard Baruch had to lose a carriage he gave his wife as a present before

---

[2] Elizabeth Fowler, *Ninety Days to Fortune* (New York: Ivan Oblensky, 1964).

[3] Charles MacKay, *Extraordinary Popular Delusions and the Madness of Crowds* (New York: Noonday Press, 1932).

he stopped risking all his capital on an investing idea. He also learned to think for himself and not to blindly follow the ideas of others, no matter how powerful or influential they might be. His greatest success came after he opened his own office strictly for himself and operated as a "lone wolf," as he called it.

This book has been designed to permit an interested reader to become a self-sufficient investor in options. He is given the basic option strategies along with a description of the skills needed to be successful. He is presented with a set of sound rules to wisely manage his capital according to the strategy he employs. It is hoped that he will learn to follow the soundness of his own ideas rather than the follies of the market crowd around him. If he follows these guidelines and does his investing homework, while he may not have an easy path to riches, he at least should possess the best chance for success.

The Fungible Option

2

The Chicago Board Options Exchange has launched a new era in stock market investing. By introducing the fungible[1] option they have not only provided a new money management tool in and of itself, but they have elevated investing in common stocks to a new level of sophistication. Just as man progressed from out of the cave to far more protection against the storms of nature, the fungible option provides protection against the vagaries of price disturbances. But, although this new type of option possesses many positive characteristics by itself, it needs many supporting tools in order to produce the profits that are possible to attain. Timing can be a factor of utmost importance, how to measure option premiums another, the relationship between the change in option premiums with the underlying stock still another. To many these are esoteric subjects. They provide a great area for mathematicians to develop measuring devices. What this book will attempt is to offer the reader a down-to-earth approach to these important matters. While the techniques developed

---

[1] As will be seen in the discussion that follows, *fungible* means "mutually interchangeable."

can be applied to stock market investing in general, they are particularly important for success in investing with options. They are the heart of the book.

Before I describe these methods and how to use them, my first order of business will be to provide the necessary background in terms of definitions and the operation of an options exchange, in this case the Chicago Board Options Exchange. While there may be some differences between it and the American, PBW, Pacific Coast, and Midwest Stock Exchange versions, the CBOE is the pilot model which has shown the way for its followers. The common ground for all the options exchanges is one clearing corporation for all options, standard terms for the options traded, and uniform margin and trading rules. The one major difference is that the PBW and American Stock Exchange, or AMEX, use the standard specialist system currently employed by the New York Stock Exchange in its stock transactions. The CBOE is unique in its use of board brokers executing public orders coupled with market makers executing their own orders plus directed orders. This feature will be more fully explained later in the chapter.

The fungibility attribute was achieved mainly through the design of a clearing corporation which acts as a guarantor of all options traded. By seeing to it that all contracts are honored, the clearing corporation provides a means to resell a purchased option to another buyer through the clearing corporation mechanism. Likewise, a seller can repurchase an identical option and thus terminate or close out his obligation. This is permissible because the option contracts traded are standardized in terms of the underlying stock, the expiration dates of the options, and the strike prices. What this can mean in terms of strategies will be covered later, but first the basic definitions and terms for this new field. The following glossary is extracted from the Options Clearing Corporation prospectus dated October 29, 1976.

Exchange-Traded Options; Put Options; Call Options—The common sense of options is that there is an option to buy or own stock (a Call) and an option to sell or dispose of stock (a Put). In the case of an owned Call option, the owner can exercise his option by delivering an exercise notice to the Clearing Corporation through his broker, with the Clearing Corporation delivering the acquired stock to the exercisor. For a Put option, the Clearing Corporation will accept delivery of the shares the Put owner is desiring to sell as an exercise of his Put option. In each case, the exchange with the Clearing Corporation due to an exercise is accomplished at the exercise price stated in the option description prior to the expiration of the option. These factors are known from the standardized description of an exchange-traded option. The designation of an Option includes the name of the underlying security, the expiration month, the exercise price, and whether the Option is a Put or a Call (e.g., XYZ July 50 Call or XYZ April 60 Put).

Underlying Security—The security subject to being purchased or sold upon the exercise of an Option.

Class of Options—Options of the same type (either a Put or a Call) covering the same underlying security (i.e., all XYZ Calls or XYZ Puts).

Series of Options—Options of the same class but also having the same exercise price, expiration time,

GLOSSARY OF TERMS

and the same unit of trading, usually 100 shares of the underlying stock.

Unit of Trading—The number of units of the underlying security designated by the Clearing Corporation as the subject of a single Option. In the absence of any other designation, the unit of trading for common stock is 100 shares. This may be adjusted for stock splits or stock dividends which might occur during the life of an option.

Exercise Price—The price per unit of the underlying security at which the holder of an Option may purchase or sell the underlying security upon exercise. The exercise price is generally termed *the strike price.*

Expiration Time—The latest time in the expiration month when an Option may be exercised at the Clearing Corporation. The exercise notice must be received at the Clearing Corporation prior to 2:00 P.M. Pacific Time, 4:00 P.M. Central Time, or 5:00 P.M. Eastern Time, on the Saturday immediately following the third Friday of the expiration month. This time should not be confused with the earlier exercise cutoff time which is the latest time a customer may inform his broker he wishes to exercise an option. This time is 2:30 P.M. Pacific Time, 4:30 P.M. Central Time, 5:30 P.M. Eastern Time on the business day immediately preceding the expiration date. It is of utmost importance for a customer to determine the cutoff time set by the broker, as it may be somewhat earlier than the times just mentioned.

Premium—The price of an Option agreed upon between the buyer and writer or their agents in a transaction on the floor of an Exchange.

Opening Purchase Transaction—A transaction in which an investor intends to become the owner of an Option.

Opening Sale Transaction—A transaction in which an investor intends to become the writer of an option.

Closing Purchase Transaction—A transaction in which an investor who is obligated as a writer of an option intends to terminate his obligation as a writer. This is accomplished by "purchasing" an Option of the same series as the Option previously written. Such a transaction has the effect, upon acceptance by the Clearing Corporation, of canceling the investor's preexisting position as a writer, instead of resulting in the issuance of an Option to the investor.

Closing Sale Transaction—A transaction in which an investor who is the holder of an unexpired Option intends to liquidate his position as a holder. This is accomplished by "selling" in a closing sale transaction an Option of the same series as the Option previously purchased. Such a transaction has the effect of liquidating the investor's preexisting position as a holder of the Option instead of resulting in the investor assuming the obligation of a writer.

Covered Put Writer—A writer of a Put, who, so long as he remains obligated as a writer, holds on a share-for-share basis, a Put of the same class as the Put written where the exercise price of the Put held is equal to or greater than the exercise price of the Put written. Note: Under exchange rules, being short the underlying security does constitute a covered writing position for margin purposes.

Covered Call Writer—A writer of a Call, who so long as he remains obligated as a writer, owns the share or other units of underlying security covered by the Call, or holds on a share-for-share basis a Call of the same class as the Call written where the exercise price of the Call held is equal to or less than the exercise price of the Call written.

Uncovered Writer—A writer of an Option who is neither short nor long the underlying security covered by the Option written.

Clearing Member—A member of an exchange who has become a clearing member of the Clearing Corporation.

Straddle—A combination of a Put and a Call Option of the same series in an underlying security, i.e., the Call and the Put have the same expiration date and exercise price for a particular underlying security.

Strip—A combination of two Puts and a Call of the same series for a particular underlying security.

Strap—A combination of two Calls and a Put of the same series for a particular underlying security.

The Clearing Corporation mentioned in the above definitions is an integral part of the exchange mechanism and a feature which offers great advantages over the OTC (over-the-counter)[2] option market. The Clearing Corporation is the obligor of all the options traded in the option auction market. The Clearing Corporation handles the accounting of the option trades between members of the Exchange, supervises the capital requirements of its members, and issues the exercise notices to its members when options are exercised; the members are then obliged to assign the exercise notices on a consistent basis to their customers. This procedure removes the one-on-one linkage between an individual buyer of an option and an individual writer which

---

[2] A complete description of the OTC option market is included in the appendix.

characterizes the OTC market. (Breaking this direct linkage between buyer and seller avoids the often sticky problem of a seller's wanting a buyer to exercise, but the buyer's refusing, even if it is to his advantage. Where the seller wanted the opportunity to unwind a position and open a new one, he was often frustrated. Worse yet, if the underlying stock began a sharp decline and the writer wanted to back out of his obligation, he couldn't. He was locked in.)

Another important Clearing Corporation feature is the collective backing of all option contracts by the Clearing Corporation members. Besides the minimum capital requirements of $150,000 or 8⅓ percent of its aggregate indebtedness, whichever is greater, each member must contribute an initial deposit of $10,000 to a clearing fund. This deposit is increased each quarter if necessary to maintain it at a level of $10 times the average daily number of open option positions. In case a member firm fails to discharge an obligation rising from a trade on an option exchange within 24 hours, his deposit is applied to discharge the obligation. If this deposit is insufficient to cover the amount, all remaining members are charged for the still outstanding amount on a pro-rata basis. If their Clearing Fund deposits are reduced because of this assessment, they must be promptly brought back to the required level. In addition, every option traded is fully margined by 9 A.M. Central Time the next morning. (By contrast, the OTC option is merely guaranteed by the New York Stock Exchange member who has handled the writer's side of the transaction. If he defaults, and the firm goes into bankruptcy, the buyer may get only partial fulfillment of the contract, and then only after lengthy legal proceedings. Because of this arrangement, experienced option traders pay particular attention during precarious stock market conditions to the identity of the firm on the other side of their option transactions.)

The proof of the exchange-traded option's superiority to the OTC option market is the fact that all OTC trading in calls also traded on the CBOE, as the first option exchange, virtually disappeared the moment CBOE trading began. The CBOE began operation on April 26, 1973, trading exclusively in call options for 16 underlying stocks. Put options began trading on June 3, 1977. The underlying stocks which qualify for options trading on the CBOE must conform to the following qualifications: (*a*) they must have a minimum of 10,000,000 shares outstanding, at least 8,000,000 of which are (according to reports filed with the SEC) beneficially owned by persons other than officers or directors of the issuer or 10-percent stockholders; (*b*) trading volume on the principal securities exchange on which the stock is listed of at least 1,000,000 shares per year in each of the two previous calendar years; and (*c*) a market price of at least $10 per share.

Less than 250 stocks can pass these strict guidelines, and the greatest majority of them are listed on the New York Stock Exchange. Other options exchanges may differ slightly in their listing requirements, but the CBOE requirements offer an excellent example of the strictness of the guidelines. Besides the requirement that all companies so qualifying to the above requirements conform to all SEC reporting regulations, each company must meet the following requirements:

1. a majority of the existing board of directors of the issuer have been directors of the issuer or a predecessor of the issuer from the beginning of the issuer's last three fiscal years;

2. the issuer and its subsidiaries have not during the past ten years defaulted in the payment of any dividend or sinking fund installment on preferred stock, or in the payment of any principal, interest, or sinking fund installment on any indebtedness for borrowed money, or in the payment of rentals under long-term leases;

3. the issuer and its consolidated subsidiaries had a net income, after taxes but before extraordinary items net of tax effect, of at least $500,000 for each of the last three fiscal years;

4. the issuer earned in each of the last five fiscal years any dividends, including the fair market value of any stock dividends, paid in each such year on all classes of securities.

The CBOE may make exceptions to one or more of the above requirements, or may continue to trade in options of the underlying stocks even though the issuer might fail in the future to meet these requirements. These stringent listing requirements are also in sharp contrast to OTC options. Because a buyer of an OTC call has to attain a price move in the underlying stock equal to the premium he paid just to break even, he has a bias to deal in the most volatile, speculative stocks he can find. For this reason OTC call writers are forced to deal in these potentially troublesome issues. The option exchanges, by dealing in the most widely held stocks and by providing the liquidity of its aftermarket, allows both writer and buyer to deal in issues least likely to incur unpleasant fundamental surprises. As of May 1, 1977, the CBOE was trading in the underlying securities listed in Table 2–1. Some options are traded on more than one exchange. This practice will become more widespread over time until quite possibly the more active options will be traded on all exchanges.

The yield of each stock is included to demonstrate another important feature of exchange-traded calls: the writer's claim to all stock dividends. If a call is exercised, the buyer takes delivery of the stock free of any dividends that go ex prior to exercise. This makes a great deal of sense, since the writer has the orientation of making a certain return on his capital, which is usually tied up in the stock used to guarantee the calls he writes. While the average yield was below the yield of the Dow Jones Industrial Average, 3.7 for CBOE versus 4.6 for the DJIA as of May 1, 1977, there were a number of stocks such as American Telephone, Exxon, Ford, General Motors, INA, IT&T and

TABLE 2–1

Underlying Stocks on the CBOE as of May 1, 1977

Stock	Yield (percent)
American Electric Power	8.4
American Hospital Supply	2.4
American Telephone & Telegraph	6.7
Aluminum Co. of America	2.5
AMP, Inc.	1.8
Atlantic Richfield	2.8
Avon Products	4.4
Bankamerica	3.3
Baxter Laboratories	0.8
Bethlehem Steel	5.7
Black & Decker	3.0
Boeing	3.0
Boise Cascade	3.4
Brunswick	4.2
Burlington Northern	3.2
Burroughs	1.4
CBS	3.4
Citicorp	3.9
Coca-Cola	4.2
Colgate-Palmolive	3.6
Commonwealth Edison	8.4
Control Data Corp.	—
Delta Airlines	2.1
Digital Equipment	—
Disney	0.5
Dow Chemical Co.	2.8
DuPont	4.0
Eastman Kodak	3.4
Exxon	5.8
Federal National Mtg.	6.2
Fluor	2.7
Ford Motors	7.3
General Dynamics	—
General Electric	3.4
General Foods	5.1
General Motors	8.2
Great Western Financial	3.0
Gulf & Western	4.9
Halliburton	1.7
Hewlett Packard	0.6

TABLE 2-1 (*continued*)

Stock	Yield (percent)
Holiday Inns	4.0
Homestake Mining	2.5
Honeywell	3.2
Houston Oil	1.8
IBM	3.8
INA	5.3
International Flavors	2.4
International Harvestor	5.0
International Minerals	5.9
International Paper	3.4
ITT	5.3
Johnson & Johnson	2.2
Kennecott Copper	2.1
Kerr-McGee	1.9
Kresge	1.9
Loews	3.7
Manville, Johns-	4.1
McDonalds	0.3
Merck	2.2
Merrill Lynch	4.9
MGIC	1.4
Minnesota Mining & Mfg	3.5
Mobil Oil	5.8
Monsanto	3.9
National Semi-Conductor	—
NCR Inc	2.4
Northwest Airlines	2.0
Occidental Petroleum	4.5
Pennzoil	4.6
Pepsico	3.4
Polaroid	1.5
Raytheon	3.3
RCA	4.1
Reynolds, R. J	5.1
Schlumberger	1.3
Sears Roebuck	3.7
Skyline	2.4
Southern Company	9.2
Sperry Rand	2.7
Standard Oil of Indiana	4.9
Syntex	2.8
Tandy	—

TABLE 2–1 (*concluded*)

Stock	Yield (percent)
Teledyne	—
Tesoro Petroleum	7.8
Texasgulf	4.4
Texas Instruments	1.6
UAL, Inc.	2.9
United Technologies	4.7
Upjohn	3.4
Walter, Jim	3.7
Weyerhaeuser	2.0
Williams Companies	4.2
Xerox	2.6
Average Yield	3.7

Mobil Oil which yielded in excess of 5 percent.

The OTC option market, surprisingly, has a dividend rule exactly opposite to that of the CBOE. Upon exercise, the OTC buyer takes delivery of his stock with all dividend rights incurred during the option period.

At the beginning of the chapter it was mentioned that the CBOE had created an aftermarket for their options by standardizing the strike prices and expiration dates of their options. This was accomplished at the outset by establishing the end of January, April, July, and October as standard expiration dates. At any one point in time there were three outstanding time periods, so that, as of February 1, there would be three-month, six-month and nine-month options trading. As time passes, the time to maturity gradually dwindles until the three-month option expires and a new nine-month option begins trading.

The standard strike or exercise prices are determined at five-point intervals for stock prices below 50, at ten-point intervals for stocks trading between 50 and 100, and 20-point intervals for stocks trading above 100. If the stock trades at a new price level falling within the strike price guidelines, a new option will usually begin trading at that level.

Since the key variables describing an exchange-traded option are its strike price and its expiration date, these elements form the standard label for a given option. An "Atlantic Richfield July 100 Call" designates the underlying stock, the expiration date, strike price, and the type of option. The standard newspaper quotes from *The Wall Street Journal* organize this information as shown in Figure 2–1.

They present the underlying stock with the strike price adjacent to it. Then, in three sets of columns to the right they present the volume in terms of options traded and the closing premium for the near- mid- and far-term contracts. The closing price for the underlying stock is presented at the last column on the right.

The next logical question should be, how are the option premiums determined? This subject will be covered completely in the following chapter on pricing tradeable options.

Once we know how much to pay or obtain in premiums for an option, the next area of investigation should be trading. Again, the CBOE has conceived an excellent design. In order to produce the liquidity which characterizes the CBOE, an ingenious system was devised. It is a hybrid

FIGURE 2–1

Chicago Board

			– Jul –		– Oct –		– Jan –		N.Y.
Option	&	price	Vol.	Last	Vol.	Last	Vol.	Last	Close
Dow Ch		30	b	b	107	2⅞	b	b	b
Alcoa		50	43	1¾	a	a	11	4½	51¾
Alcoa		60	a	a	2	5-16	a	a	51¾
Am Exp		35	5	4½	113	5⅝	103	6¼	39⅝
Am Exp		40	122	1-16	11	1⅝	5	2¼	39⅝
Am Tel		55	5	7½	b	b	b	b	62½
Am Tel		60	99	2½	37	3⅛	26	3⅜	62½
Am Tel		65	a	a	100	7-16	59	1	62½
Atl R		50	274	8⅝	341	9¾	14	10¾	58⅝
Atl R		60	294	1-16	1117	2 11-16	312	3¾	58⅝
Avon		40	80	9¾	b	b	b	b	49½
Avon		45	236	4⅝	28	5⅛	12	5⅞	49½
Avon	p	45	b	b	28	9-16	26	1⅛	49½
Avon		50	806	¼	299	2	47	2⅞	49½
Avon	p	50	b	b	57	2¼	35	3¼	49½
BankAm		20	8	4	8	4	13	4¾	23⅞
BankAm		25	50	1-16	106	11-16	100	1⅛	23⅞
Beth S		30	b	b	48	1 9-16	34	2⅛	30¼
Beth S		35	a	a	115	5-16	70	⅝	30¼
Beth S		40	a	a	70	1-16	70	¼	30¼
Bruns		15	9	1-16	58	½	92	13-16	14
Burl N		40	7	9⅞	a	a	b	b	49⅞
Burl N		45	90	4⅞	14	5⅞	3	7	49⅞
Burl N		50	182	⅜	92	2½	51	3½	49⅞
Burrgh		50	51	12½	32	12¾	10	13¼	62⅜
Burrgh		60	488	2 13-16	66	5	22	7	62⅜
Burrgh		70	a	a	122	1⅛	9	2¼	62⅜
Burrgh		80	a	a	8	⅛	b	b	62⅜
Citicp		25	115	2¾	21	3⅛	10	3¾	27⅝
Citicp		30	20	1-16	61	½	45	1	27⅝
Delta		30	12	4⅞	a	a	a	a	35
Delta		35	91	¼	14	1¾	3	2⅜	35
Delta		40	1	1-16	95	⅜	11	⅞	35
Dig Eq		35	90	11⅛	1	11⅝	21	11½	45⅞
Dig Eq		40	340	6⅛	55	7¼	18	8⅛	45⅞
Dig Eq		45	836	1 5-16	125	3¾	88	5⅛	45⅞
Dig Eq		46⅝	900	5-16	b	b	b	b	45⅞
Dig Eq		50	60	1-16	226	1 9-16	152	2¾	45⅞
Dig Eq		60	a	a	10	3-16	b	b	45⅞
Disney		30	b	b	22	6¼	15	7	35⅞
Disney		35	108	1	106	2 9-16	28	3⅜	35⅞
Disney		40	a	a	69	⅝	153	1⅜	35⅞
Dow Ch		30	b	b	b	b	559	3⅝	31¾
Dow Ch		35	12	1-16	304	¾	696	1 7-16	31¾
Dow Ch		40	6	1-16	22	⅛	39	⅜	31¾
Dow Ch		45	a	a	22	1-16	b	b	31¾
du Pnt		110	b	b	19	7⅛	2	9	114¼
du Pnt		120	50	1-16	86	2⅜	40	4⅛	114¼
du Pnt		130	a	a	391	7-16	107	1½	114¼
du Pnt		140	a	a	200	⅛	b	b	114¼
Eas Kd		50	b	b	112	9	24	9⅞	58¼
Eas Kd	p	50	b	b	177	⅜	67	1 1-16	58¼
Eas Kd		60	1424	1-16	699	2⅝	202	4	58¼
Eas Kd	p	60	b	b	315	4	48	4⅞	58¼
Eas Kd		70	a	a	460	7-16	683	1 1-16	58¼
Eas Kd		80	a	a	3	⅛	b	b	58¼

Listed Options Quotations

Wednesday, July 13, 1977

Closing prices of all options. Sales unit usually is 100 shares. Security description includes exercise price. Stock close is New York Stock Exchange final price. p-Put option.

			– Jul –		– Oct –		– Jan –		N.Y.
Option	&	price	Vol.	Last	Vol.	Last	Vol.	Last	Close
Teldyn		60	261	10½	108	12½	2	13¼	70⅞
Teldyn		68	562	2¾	81	6⅜	b	b	70⅞
Teldyn		70	1331	1⅛	313	5¼	246	7⅛	70⅞
Tesoro		10	128	4⅜	128	4½	55	4½	14½
Tesoro		15	54	1-16	277	⅝	397	1	14½
Tex In		80	202	10	57	10¼	14	13¼	90
Tex In		90	660	⅝	163	4⅝	116	6⅞	90
Tex In		100	10	1-16	256	1 3-16	b	b	90
Upjohn		30	53	3½	22	3¾	12	4⅜	33⅝
Upjohn		35	11	1-16	203	13-16	39	1⅜	33⅝
Upjohn		40	a	a	10	⅛	b	b	33⅝
Weyerh		30	b	b	38	3	3	3½	32
Weyerh		35	b	b	72	11-16	143	1⅜	32
Weyerh		40	a	a	118	¼	31	½	32
Xerox		45	1008	5⅛	429	6¼	399	7¼	50¼
Xerox		50	5814	9-16	1799	2 15-16	678	4	50¼
Xerox		60	13	1-16	216	5-16	b	b	50¼
			– Aug –		– Nov –		– Feb –		
A E P		19⅞	26	5¼	15	5⅜	a	a	25
A E P		24⅞	261	⅜	179	⅝	46	11-16	25
Am Hos		25	a	a	4	15-16	a	a	23⅝
Bally		20	338	2 3-16	281	3⅜	90	4	21½
Bally		25	750	⅜	510	1¼	242	1⅞	21½
Bally		30	a	a	86	⅜	b	b	21½
Baxter		30	2	3⅛	a	a	a	a	33¼
Baxter		35	6	⅜	39	1⅜	a	a	33¼
Blk Dk		15	34	15-16	150	1½	166	1¾	15½
Blk Dk		20	21	1-16	139	3-16	28	7-16	15½
Boeing		40	37	16⅛	a	a	b	b	56
Boeing		45	34	11⅜	13	11½	b	b	56
Boeing		50	114	6½	64	7⅝	12	8¾	56
Boeing		60	216	13-16	167	2⅜	46	3⅜	56
Bois C		25	a	a	35	3	a	a	27
Bois C		30	43	¼	30	¾	106	1¼	27
Bois C		35	3	1-16	59	¼	a	a	27
C B S		60	30	1⅛	41	2⅛	15	3	59¾
Coke		35	67	3½	25	3¾	10	4⅜	38¼
Coke		40	184	5-16	151	13-16	33	1½	38¼

Courtesy of Dow Jones and Co.

of the New York Stock Exchange specialist system and the over-the-counter securities markets. Rather than having a stock assigned to one specialist, who then supposedly buys and sells stock against the tide of broker orders, the CBOE has a board broker who handles *only* customers' orders. He buys and sells no options for his own account as a New York Stock Exchange specialist would. The CBOE board broker keeps a book of all customer orders for which *no* member firm or market maker orders are entered. The market maker represents the other part of the CBOE hybrid system. He is allowed to buy and sell options for his own account *only*. He can quote his trades within a point range of the board broker, but if he is quoting a premium either on the buy or sell side at the same price as the board broker, the board broker's trades take *priority*. With this set of operating rules the thorny specialist problem has been solved in favor of the individual customer. His orders take priority over the "insiders" or market makers. In a world where many people have grown cynical about the unfairness of the "system," the CBOE has bent over backwards for the individual investor.

The AMEX employs the standard specialist system, which has a great drawback of less liquidity than the CBOE system followed by the Midwest and Pacific Coast Exchanges. For execution purposes, liquidity is of paramount importance. As dually listed trading among the various option exchanges, the CBOE model should easily prove its superiority, thereby capturing the lion's share of dually listed orders.

How should orders be placed? When an individual has decided that the precise moment has arrived to either buy or sell an option, he is usually best served by obtaining a market quote and then giving himself a $\frac{1}{16}$ point leeway for options trading under $2 ($200 for a 100-share option), ⅛ leeway above 2 and below 10, and ¼ above 10. In other words, if the current bid-offer market quote is 2½ to 3, 1 by 2, this means that there is a total of orders on the board broker's book to buy at 2½ and another to sell at 3. The "1 by 2" tells you that there is one option to buy at 2½ and two options for sale at 3. If you were an anxious buyer, you would place an order to buy at 3 with ⅛ discretion. This allows your broker on the floor of the exchange to pay 3⅛ if he has to in order to complete the transaction. If you were an anxious seller instead, your ⅛ leeway (or "discretion" in auction market terms) would be used relative to the bid of 2½ so that a typical order might be to sell at 2½ with ⅛ discretion, meaning you will accept 2⅜ as your price if necessary to complete the trade.

If an investor is more patient or is not reacting to a recent news development, he should use limit orders to be placed on the board broker's book. If an investor has estimated from the behavior of the underlying stock and the premium curves introduced in the next chapter that a given option should trade in the vicinity of $3, he should place either a day order, if he is reevaluating daily, or a G.T.C. (good 'til canceled) order on the *board broker's book* (this is important) to buy or sell at a price of $3. Option premiums are volatile to the extent that an investor who chases a market—in other words he turns bullish *after* strength occurs in the market—will invariably "pay up" for all his trades. The ideal is to have some estimate of a reasonable price and attempt to trade at that level. To accomplish this requires some trading skill and price measurements. These subjects will be treated in the chapter on price behavior.

In terms of trading, an option that is initially purchased is either resold in the auction market for a profit or a loss, exercised to take delivery of the underlying stock, or allowed to expire worthless. An option initially sold (written) is either repurchased to close out the position, allowed to expire, in which case the premium is realized as a profit, or exercised, in which case the writer must honor the option obligation. Exercising is the term which describes the action of the holder of an option who decides to take advantage of the contract terms of the option he owns and take delivery in the case of a call (he "calls" for the stock) or sells stock in the case of a put (he "puts" the stock to the writer). For all practical purposes he will decide to do this only at the end of the option's life. At any time before that he is usually better off simply selling his option for a profit in the aftermarket. This is so because he incurs a brokerage commission on the 100 shares of stock involved in the exercise. If he can cash in his profits on a stock price change which occurs prior to expiration, why should he not take advantage of the opportunity? Besides this, he may not have the additional capital required to purchase the stock in the case of a call. In the case of a put, where no underlying security may be held, why should he purchase stock for resale on an exercise and incur two stock commissions?

All listed options can be exercised at any time prior to 2 P.M. Pacific Time, 4 P.M. Central Time, or 5 P.M. Eastern Time on the Saturday immediately following the third Friday of the expiration month. This time is the latest a Clearing Member may present an exercise notice to the Clearing Corporation. An individual holder of an option must instruct his broker he wishes to exercise by 2:30 P.M. Pacific Time, 4:30 P.M. Central Time, or 5:30 P.M. Eastern Time on the third Friday of the expiration month. Brokerage firms may set earlier cutoff times than this, therefore, it is imperative that a customer check this important detail with his broker in order that he does not miss the opportunity to exercise. This could be an expensive oversight.

When an exercise notice is tendered to the Clearing Corporation, it is randomly assigned by computer to a Clearing Member who has an account with the Clearing Corporation reflecting an option or options of the same denomination being exercised. If a certificate has been issued evidencing an option (this is exceptional and usually only occurs if a bank is transacting option writing in a custodial account and desires a piece of paper to assist in their bookkeeping), this certificate must accompany the exercise notice, otherwise the notice will not be accepted by the Clearing Corporation. Upon acceptance of an exercise notice and Clearing Corporation assignment of the exercise to a Clearing Member on the day following the receipt of the notice, the Clearing Member must then assign the exercise to one or more of its customers on a consistent basis which is registered with the Clearing Corporation. The method of assignment may be random selection, a "first-in, first-out" basis, or any other method that is deemed fair and equitable to a brokerage firm's customers. The "first-in, first-out" approach has some serious drawbacks in that a particular option writer who tends to write far-out options, in order to achieve larger premiums, may suffer a penalty of receiving a disproportionate number of exercise notices. The fairest method known to the author is that employed by Cowen & Company, whereby each option contract in-house is assigned a number. Exercise notices are then assigned among the available options at random, using these numbers. In this manner large accounts are not penalized by an above average number of exercises, as can occur on a "first-in, first-out" method. Serious option writers should inquire about such details before they open a new account with any brokerage firm.

The commissions charged by Clearing Corporation members vary a great deal since the May 1, 1975, termination of fixed commissions by the SEC. The following table gives the typical commission formulas used by large nondiscount retail-oriented brokerage firms. They are involved enough that computers are relied on to determine the appropriate amount and then print the statement of the trade, or confirm, sent to each customer. Discount brokerage firms that stress execution alone may offer rates 30 to 40 percent below the rates computed from the commission table (Table 2–2).

For a typical example, suppose a customer purchased a single IBM April 260 Call option at $18 (or $1,800). To compute the commission charge, enter the commission table at the section entitled Single option. The principal amount is the total dollars involved in the trade prior to commissions. In our case of $1,800, we take 1.3 percent of $1,800, or $23.40 from column 1 and add the $12.00 amount from column 2, for a total charge of $35.40. If the transaction were a sale, SEC fees of one cent for every $300 of principal would be involved. New York State transfer taxes do not apply to options.

If the order for five of the same IBM options were entered, the commissions computation would be more involved as follows:

1. The principal amount is now five times $1,800, or $9,000. Therefore, the entry for column 1 is 0.9 percent times $9,000, or $81.00.
2. To that is added $22.00 from column 2, for a subtotal of $103.00.
3. To this subtotal is added $6.00 per contract for the five contracts, or $30.00, for a new subtotal of $133.00.
4. Then a charge of 15 percent is added to this subtotal (or $133.00 times 0.15), for $19.95, bringing the subtotal to $152.95.
5. The final charge of 8 percent is applied to the $152.95 subtotal, for a $12.24 charge. The total commission charge is therefore $165.19.

TABLE 2-2

	Principal from: But Less than	(1) Percent of Principal	(2) Plus	(3) Plus	(4) Plus Percent of Commission (1)+(2)+(3)	(5) Plus Percent of Commission (1)+(2)+(3)+(4)
Stock, warrants, rights—						
Single round lot (over $1/share)	100– 800	2.0%	6.40		10%	8% (Retail only)
	800– 2,500	1.3	12.00		10	8 (Retail only)
	2,500– 5,000	0.9	22.00		10	8 (Retail only)
	5,001 and above	0.9	22.00		15	8
Multiple round lots (over $1/share)	100– 2,500	1.3	12.00	$6.00/Round lots for 1st ten Round lots	10	8 (Retail only)
	2,500– 5,000	0.9	22.00		10	8 (Retail only)
	5,001– 20,000	0.9	22.00		15	8
	20,000– 30,000	0.6	82.00	$4.00/Round lot for 11th and above	15	8
	30,000 and above	0.4	142.00		15	8
Odd lots and partial round lots	Under $100	8.4				
	100– 800	2.0	4.40		10	8
	800– 2,500	1.3	10.00		10	8
	2,500– 5,000	0.9	20.00		10	8
	5,001 and above	0.9	20.00		15	8
Under $1.00	0– 100	8.4			10	8 (Retail only)
	1,000– 2,500	5.0	34.00		10	8 (Retail only)
	5,001– 10,000	5.0	34.00		15	8
	10,000 and above	4.0	134.00		15	8
Options: Under $1.00	All amounts	—	*$6.25 per/option			
Options ASE/CBOE/PBW options Single option	0– 100	8.4				
	100– 2,500	1.3	12.00			
	2,500 and above	0.9	22.00			

Multiple options

100–	2,500	1.3	12.00	$6.00/Contract for 1st ten contracts	10	8
2,500–	5,000	0.9	22.00		10	8
5,001–	20,000	0.9	22.00	$4.00/Contract for 11th and above	15	8
20,000	and above	0.6	82.00		15	8

Bonds

0–	49	$7.50/Bond
50–	99	5.00/Bond
100M and above		2.50/Bond

Note: All commission calculations are based upon an order; all transactions for one account for the same security, same side, the same day unless otherwise specified.

Minimum commission
  1. Retail accounts (stock only)—$20.00 or 10 percent of the principal, whichever is less.
  2. Options over $1.00 = $25.00 minimum.
*3. If option price is 1/16 or less, 50 percent of principal is taken.

Maximum commission
  1. Principal under $5,000—Retail accounts—$77.22/Round lot.
  2. Principal $5,000 or greater—$80.73/Round lot.

While all these steps may seem staggering, the per contract charge is $33.04, slightly less than the $35.40 single contract. The additional steps for multiple options are necessary to compensate for the extra bookkeeping involved, especially in the case the option exercise process is involved.

In all cases, however, the minimum commission on an option costing more than $1.00 ($100 for the option) is $25.00. For a cost of $\frac{1}{16}$ or less ($6.25 or less) the minimum is 50 percent of the principal. In some cases this can be negotiated.

Margin requirements are uniform for all the approved options exchanges and are as follows:

1. All purchases of options must be paid for in cash within one business day of the trade. The options have no loan value in a margin account.

2. All opening sales (writing of options) where the underlying stock is owned by the investor require no margin. The only limitation is that when valuing the equity in the account, the equity value of the stock cannot exceed the exercise value of the option written.

3. The uncovered writing of calls is subject to the following rules:

    a. The rules are based on the value of the underlying security.

        (1) 30 percent of the value of the underlying security is required. (Some brokers may require as much as 50 percent.)

        (2) Margin is increased or decreased

by the amount the option is in-the-money (stock price is above the strike price) or is decreased by the amount the option is out-of-the-money (the stock price is below the strike price).

(3) Minimum margin is $250 per contract.

(4) The original premium received reduces the initial margin requirement.

4. The uncovered writing of puts is subject to the following rules, also based on the value of the underlying security:

   a. 30 percent of the value of the underlying security is required. (Some brokers may require as much as 50 percent).

   b. Margin is increased by the amount the option is in-the-money (stock price is below the strike price) or is decreased by the amount the option is out-of-the-money (the stock price is above the strike price).

   c. Minimum margin is $250 per contract.

   d. The original premium received reduces the initial margin requirement.

5. The uncovered writing of straddles (short call–short put) requires evaluating each side of the straddle based on the margin requirements given in 3 and 4 above. Whichever option requires the greater margin, put or call, that option determines the minimum requirement for the straddle.

   a. If an investor owns underlying stock and writes a straddle, no margin is required for the call side, but the put is considered uncovered unless an offsetting long put of equal or greater strike price and at least equal life is also owned.

b. If an investor is short stock and writes a straddle, he will be required to meet the minimum margin requirement for the short stock in addition to the regular margin requirement for the naked call. By option exchange rules, and this is important, a put is considered covered if the customer is also short the shares of the underlying security.

EXAMPLE

To write an Atlantic Richfield 100 call option naked with a premium of $900 and a price for the underlying stock of 95, the margin would be as follows:

30% times the market value of the underlying stock.....................	$2,850
Less out-of-the-money amount............	−500
Margin Required.....................	$2,350
Less the option premium received........	−900
Additional cash margin needed..........	$1,450

If the stock price moved up 10 points to 105, the margin calculation for a "mark to the market" would be as follows:

30% times the market value of the underlying stock.....................	$3,150
Plus in-the-money value.................	+500
Margin Required.....................	$3,650

Note: Where the stock value has appreciated $1,000 the margin requirement increased $1,300 from $2,350 to $3,650, or 130 percent of the increase in the underlying stock's value.

To write an Atlantic Richfield 100 put option naked with a premium of $1100 and a price for the underlying stock of $95, the margin would be as follows:

30% times the market value of the underlying stock......................	$2,850
Plus the in-the-money amount.............	+500
Margin Required......................	$3,350
Less the option premium received.........	−1,100
Additional cash margin needed.........	$2,250

If the stock price moved up 10 points to $105, the margin calculation for a "mark to the market" would be as follows:

30% times the market value of the underlying stock.......................	$3,150
Less out-of-the-money amount.............	−500
Margin Required......................	$2,650

In this case, the margin requirement dropped from $3,350 to $2,650, or $700. The change in margin requirement with a change in value of the underlying stock is less than in the case of a naked call. It is actually 70 percent of the increase in the underlying stock's value. Perhaps the reader can appreciate the importance of good bookkeeping in keeping track of option positions.

The subject of income tax will be covered briefly for the individual in order to provide the background necessary to understand the examples of strategies presented in the following chapters.

The Tax Reform Act of 1976 changed the tax laws regarding options to the extent that all profits or losses from both writing and purchase of options are of a capital nature. For the tax year of 1977, the holding period for a long-term capital gain is for more than 9 months. After December 31, 1977, the holding period is more than 12 months. Unless option terms are extended beyond 9 months, then 12-month holding periods, long-term capital gains will not be possible with options.

For the purchase of call options, the capital gains treatment would be as follows:

Stock Price Behavior	Tax Treatment*
1. Stock is up, call resold for a profit	Short-term capital gain; e.g., call purchased for $400, sold for $600 eight months later becomes a short-term capital gain of $200.
2. Stock is down, call resold at a loss†	Short-term capital loss; e.g., call purchased for $600, sold for $300 five months later becomes short-term capital loss of $300.
3. Stock is down, option expires worthless	Short-term capital loss; e.g., call purchased for $500, expires worthless in four months for a short-term capital loss of $500.
4. Stock is up, call exercised	The call premium paid is added to the price of the stock to become the cost base of the security. Commissions are included in this base. The time period for the capital gain or loss begins upon the exercise of the option; e.g., a call costing $1,000 is exercised at a strike price of $100, producing a cost basis of $110 for the stock. Holding period then begins.

* In the examples given commissions are not taken into account.
† It is possible to incur a loss in a call with the stock price unchanged simply because of passage of time.

For purposes of contrast, the corresponding put buying results are detailed as follows:

Stock Price Behavior	*Tax Treatment*
1. Stock is up, put expires worthless	Short-term capital loss, e.g., put purchased for $300, expires worthless six months later for a short term capital loss of $300.
2. Stock is down, put resold at a profit	Gain on put is a capital gain, which must be short-term under the new tax laws. For example, a put purchased for $200 is sold seven months later for $500 for a short-term capital gain of $300.
3. Stock price is down, put is exercised	In this case the cost of the put would be treated as a reduction in the proceeds of the sale of the stock delivered on exercise. If we assume a 50 strike price put costing $300 was purchased on the same day that 100 shares of the underlying stock was purchased for $46, the two are considered "married." If this stock is delivered at the option exercise six months later the holding period for the stock is not affected by the put purchase, which the IRS normally considers a holding period negating short-sale. This fact should be studied more closely in the final chapter on taxes. For our simple case we assume the cost of our stock to be $46 plus the $300 paid for the put (plus commissions, which we will ignore for simplicity sake) for a cost of $4,900. The price of 50 received upon exercise gives us a $100 short-term capital gain.
4. Stock is up, put resold at a loss.	A put purchased for $200 is sold five months later for $50 for a $150 short-term capital loss.

All possible call writing results are detailed as follows:

Stock Price Behavior	Tax Treatment*
1. Stock price is up, call repurchased at a loss	Loss on call is a capital loss, which must be short-term. For example, a call written at $300 is repurchased at $700 seven months later for a $400 short-term capital loss.
2. Stock price is up, call is exercised	Call premium is added to the proceeds of the sale at the exercise price. These proceeds are compared to the cost basis of the stock delivered on the exercise to determine the gain or loss. For example, a call written at $600 is exercised at a strike price of $50. The proceeds are $50 plus the call premium, or $56. Since the stock was purchased 13 months earlier at $40, the result is a long-term capital gain of $1,600.
3. Stock price is down, call repurchased at a gain	The gain on the call is short-term. For example, a call written at $400 is repurchased at $100 three months later for a short-term capital gain of $300.
4. Stock price is down, call expires worthless	The premium received is treated as a short-term capital gain with the assumption that the call was repurchased at zero cost on the date of expiration. For example, a call written at $700 expires worthless six months later for a short-term capital gain of $700.

The comparative results for the writing of puts is as follows:

Stock Price Behavior	Tax Treatment
1. Stock price is up, put expires worthless	The premium received is treated as a short-term capital gain with the assumption that the call was repurchased at zero cost on the date of expiration. For example, a put written at $500 expires worthless three months later for a short-term capital gain of $500.
2. Stock price is up, put repurchased at a gain	The gain on the profitable repurchase of a put is treated as a short-term capital gain. For example, a put sold at a premium of $700 is repurchased five months later at $200 for a short-term capital gain of $500.
3. Stock price is down, put is exercised	This transaction should be treated by the writer as a purchase of the underlying stock. The premium received is subtracted from the cost basis of the stock. The holding period for capital gains purposes begins with the acquisition of the stock, which, for conservative purposes should be considered as the date of acquisition of the stock if a long-term capital gain is sought. For example, a put with a strike price of $50 for which a premium of $500 was received is exercised. The cost basis of the stock is $45. If the stock was sold, 13 months after acquisition, for $60, the long-term capital gain would be $1,500.
4. Stock price is down, put repurchased at a loss	The loss on the unprofitable buy back of a put is a short-term capital loss, e.g., a put written for a premium of $500 is repurchased four months later at $800 for a short-term capital loss of $300.

Now that the background regarding exchange-traded options has been covered, the reader should be prepared for the fun part—application, the art and science of making money by the use of options.

Pricing the New Options

3

The ability to price an option is a key ingredient to success with options investing. If an investor can predetermine whether an option premium is above or below a fair economic value based on the important price determinants, he has a decided advantage over his less informed counterpart. If he is a writer he wants the fattest premiums available for several reasons, the primary one being the added profit or protection he will receive relative to his investment. But almost as important is the fact that the overvalued premium gives him an edge. If the premium returns to a more normal valuation during the life of his position, this is an additional source of profit. Other investors will have to depend solely on time and the price behavior of the underlying stock.

If an investor is a buyer, he wants the best buy for his money in terms of what he has to pay to realize a potential profit. Since leverage is important, an option purchased at $200 which rises to $400 yields a profit of 100 percent compared with the same option purchased for $250, which only yields a 60-percent result.

Another tremendous advantage is the ability

to predetermine with a high degree of accuracy what a premium might be if a stock rose 10 points in two months or declined 20 points in five months. Many such evaluations can be made before establishing a position in order to decide whether the transaction is worthwhile or not.

To provide such measurements, the top brokerage firms have commissioned consultants and developed expensive computer programs which generate such information. But, since these inputs may not be available to every reader, in order to make him self-sufficient and capable of making his own decisions, this chapter will provide him with all the premium-measuring tools he needs. The few computations are relatively simple and the rest merely is a matter of reading premium values from a set of graphs.

The important factors used to evaluate option premiums are all related to the return an option writer can expect as compensation for his tying up capital to honor the option contract and for the risk he undertakes by either owning the optioned stock or placing in reserve the cash to buy or take delivery of the stock at exercise time, if either event occurs. The usual variables used to estimate option premiums are the time remaining in the option, the stock's dividend rate, and the stock's price volatility as a proxy for risk. The first two variables are simply measured, but volatility is more of a challenge.

Burton Malkiel, author with Richard Quandt,

of a book on stock options,[1] as well as of the well-known *A Random Walk Down Wall Street*, suggests the following measure:

$$\frac{\text{Estimated}}{\text{volatility}} = \frac{\text{52-week stock price range}}{\text{Average 52-week stock price}}$$

Or, in terms of algebra,

$$\text{Estimated volatility} = \frac{H - L}{(H + L)/2}$$

where

$$H = \text{the stock's 52-week high}$$
$$L = \text{the stock's 52-week low}$$

These statistics are readily obtained from the *Media General Financial Weekly,* sold at most financial district newsstands. This book uses a variation of Malkiel's approach, which seems to relate more to a commonsense understanding of stock price behavior. Half the 52-week range is used instead of the entire range. This may seem a small difference, but the result is a volatility measure which estimates the move that a stock can be expected to have above or below its average price during a year's time. For example, a 10-percent volatility for American Telephone would suggest a high of 55 for a year if the average price were expected to be 50. In this manner the volatility of American Telephone can easily be compared to that of Polaroid, a 40-percent volatile stock on average, which would have an estimated high of 70 if the

[1] B. G. Malkiel and R. E. Quandt, *Strategies and Rational Decisions in the Securities Options Market* (Cambridge, Mass.: MIT Press, 1969).

TABLE 3–1

Exchange Tradeable Options

Underlying Stock	Price	Annual Dividend	Percent Yield	Exchanges Trading	Cycle	Percent Volatility
AMF, Inc.................	20⅝	$1.24	6.0	A	FEB	13
ASA Ltd..................	19½	0.80	4.1	A	FEB	42
Abbot Labs...............	44⅞	1.00	2.2	P	FEB	19
Aetna Life...............	31	1.20	3.9	A	JAN	20
Allied Chemical...........	45⅛	1.80	4.0	P	JAN	17
Allis Chalmers............	30¼	0.90	3.0	P	JAN	31
Alcoa....................	58¾	1.40	2.4	C	JAN	15
Amerada Hess.............	33	0.60	1.8	P	FEB	35
American Broadcasting.....	46	1.00	2.2	PC	FEB	24
American Cyanamid........	27	1.50	5.6	A	JAN	12
American Electric Power....	24¾	2.05	8.3	C	FEB	12
American Home Products...	29¼	1.10	3.8	A	JAN	15
American Hospital Supply..	25⅝	0.40	1.6	C	FEB	19
American Telephone & Telegraph...............	62¾	4.20	6.7	C	JAN	10
AMP, Inc.................	27½	0.48	1.7	C	FEB	19
ASARCO, Inc..............	21¾	0.80	3.7	A	JAN	17
Ashland Oil..............	33⅝	1.90	5.7	P	JAN	20
Atlantic Richfield..........	56¾	1.60	2.8	C	JAN	20
AVNET...................	17¾	0.60	3.4	A	FEB	17
Avon Products.............	48⅞	2.00	4.1	C	JAN	14
Bally.....................	21½	0.05	0.2	C, A	FEB	40
Bankamerica..............	25⅛	0.80	3.2	C, PC	JAN	12
Baxter Labs..............	32	0.24	0.8	C	FEB	20
Beatrice Foods.............	24⅞	0.96	3.9	A	JAN	14
Bethlehem Steel...........	36	2.00	5.6	C	JAN	16
Black & Decker...........	17	0.48	2.8	C	FEB	23
Blue Bell, Inc.............	29⅜	1.00	3.4	P	JAN	27
Boeing...................	45	1.40	3.1	C	FEB	30
Boise Cascade.............	32⅞	1.10	3.3	C, P	FEB	17
Braniff International.......	9⅜	0.24	2.6	P	JAN	22
Bristol Meyers.............	65¾	2.20	3.3	M	MAR	16
Brunswick Corp...........	15⅛	0.60	4.0	C	JAN	18
Burlington Northern........	49	1.60	3.3	C	JAN	16
Burroughs.................	61¾	0.80	1.3	A, C	JAN	28
CBS, Inc.................	60⅝	2.00	3.3	C	FEB	10
Carrier Corp..............	17¾	0.64	3.6	M	MAR	18
Caterpillar...............	57½	1.50	2.6	A	FEB	12
Champion International....	24½	1.00	4.1	M	MAR	12
Chase Manhattan..........	31⅜	2.20	7.0	A	JAN	12
Citicorp..................	29	1.06	3.7	C	JAN	15
City Investing.............	14⅞	0.80	5.4	P	JAN	34
Clorox...................	10⅜	0.52	5.0	P, PC	JAN	12
Coca-Cola.................	79⅛	2.08	2.6	C	FEB	10
Colgate Palmolive..........	25⅜	0.88	3.5	C	FEB	11
Combustion Engineering....	56½	2.00	3.5	PC	MAR	20
Commonwealth Edison.....	29⅝	2.40	8.1	C	FEB	15
Communications Satellite...	35	1.00	2.9	P	JAN	20
Con Edison...............	22½	2.00	8.9	A	FEB	18

TABLE 3–1 (*continued*)

Underlying Stock	*Price*	*Annual Dividend*	*Percent Yield*	*Exchanges Trading*	*Cycle*	*Percent Volatility*
Continental Oil	36⅞	$1.20	3.3	P	JAN	12
Continental Telephone	15⅜	1.08	7.0	A	JAN	18
Control Data	21⅞	0.15	0.7	C	FEB	15
Corning Glass	66¼	1.52	2.3	M	MAR	15
Crown Zellerbach	41	1.80	4.4	PC	JAN	30
Deere & Co.	32	1.10	3.4	A	JAN	16
Delta Airlines	33¼	0.70	2.1	C	JAN	20
Diamond Shamrock	36¾	1.10	3.0	PC	JAN	14
Digital Equipment	39½	None	—	A, C	JAN	20
Disney	35⅝	0.16	0.4	A, C, PC	JAN	26
Dr. Pepper	12	0.44	3.7	A	FEB	22
Dow Chemical	38⅝	1.00	2.6	C	JAN	21
Dresser Industries	44	0.80	1.8	P	JAN	14
DuPont	129	5.00	3.9	A, C	JAN	14
Duke Power	21¾	1.60	7.5	P	JAN	17
Eastern Gas & Fuel	27½	0.80	2.9	P	JAN	36
Eastman Kodak	70	1.60	2.3	C	JAN	27
El Paso Co.	15¾	1.10	7.2	A	FEB	13
Englehard Minerals	36½	1.20	3.3	P	JAN	15
Evans Products	12¾	0.60	4.9	M	MAR	26
Exxon	52⅝	3.00	5.7	C	JAN	12
Federal Nat. Mtg.	16½	1.00	6.1	C	JAN	13
Federated Dept. Stores	41	1.46	3.6	PC	FEB	20
Firestone	20	1.10	5.5	P	FEB	13
First Charter Financial	18⅛	0.60	3.3	A	JAN	21
Fleetwood	12½	0.40	3.2	A	FEB	27
Fluor Corp.	35⅜	1.00	2.8	C	JAN	20
Ford Motor	56⅞	3.20	5.6	C	JAN	8
Freeport Minerals	27¼	1.60	5.9	M	MAR	12
GAF Corp.	11⅜	0.60	5.3	P	JAN	20
General Dynamics	54¼	None	—	C	FEB	20
General Electric	53¾	1.80	3.3	C	JAN	8
General Foods	31⅝	1.64	5.2	C	FEB	14
General Motors	69½	5.80	8.3	C	JAN	11
General Telephone & Electronics	30	2.00	6.7	A	JAN	15
Georgia Pacific	33⅜	0.80	2.4	P	JAN	13
Gillette	28	1.50	5.4	A	JAN	15
Goodyear	20	1.10	5.5	A	JAN	11
W. R. Grace & Co.	28⅞	1.70	5.9	A	FEB	12
Great Western Financial	24⅞	0.50	2.0	C	JAN	22
Greyhound	14⅜	1.04	7.2	A	JAN	10
Gulf & Western Ind.	14⅛	0.66	4.7	C	JAN	24
Gulf Oil	29⅜	1.08	3.7	A	JAN	13
Halliburton	60⅛	1.00	1.7	C	JAN	18
Hercules	24¼	1.00	4.1	A	JAN	22
Heublein	26⅛	1.32	5.1	PC	FEB	37
Hewlett Packard	74⅞	0.40	0.5	C	FEB	26
Hilton Hotels	23	0.92	4.0	PC	FEB	22
Holiday Inns	12⅜	0.46	3.7	C	FEB	16
Homestake Mining	40¼	1.00	2.5	C	JAN	28

TABLE 3–1 (*continued*)

Underlying Stock	Price	Annual Dividend	Percent Yield	Exchanges Trading	Cycle	Percent Volatility
Honeywell................	48½	$ 1.60	3.3	C	FEB	14
Household Finance.........	20	1.20	6.0	A	JAN	21
Houston Oil..............	44	0.80	1.8	C, PC	JAN	53
Howard Johnson...........	10⅛	0.32	3.2	P	JAN	22
Hughes Tool..............	38⅝	0.50	1.3	M	MAR	21
INA Corp.................	42¼	2.30	5.4	C	JAN	16
Inexco Oil................	20	None	—	P	FEB	44
IBM.....................	272½	10.00	3.7	C	JAN	8
International Flavors.......	20⅜	0.44	2.2	C	FEB	20
International Harvester.....	35½	1.85	5.2	C	JAN	19
International Minerals......	41	2.40	5.9	C	JAN	14
International Paper........	58½	2.00	3.4	C	JAN	20
International Telephone & Telegraph...............	33½	1.76	5.3	C	JAN	17
Johns Manville............	35	1.40	4.0	C	FEB	16
Johnson & Johnson.........	67¾	1.10	1.6	C	JAN	19
Joy Mfg..................	47⅞	1.30	2.7	P	FEB	16
Kennecott................	27½	0.60	2.2	C	JAN	18
Kerr-McGee..............	65⅞	1.25	1.9	C	JAN	16
Kresge...................	32¼	0.32	1.0	C	JAN	16
Levi Strauss..............	28	0.80	2.9	PC	JAN	24
Lilly, Eli.................	43⅝	1.42	3.3	A	JAN	18
Litton Industries..........	14⅝	Stock only	—	M	MAR	28
Loews Corp...............	34⅜	1.20	3.5	C	JAN	20
Louisiana Land...........	27⅜	1.20	4.4	P	FEB	15
Louisiana Pacific..........	16¼	0.20	1.2	A	FEB	20
Lucky Stores.............	15¼	0.68	4.5	PC	MAR	12
MGIC...................	15⅜	0.20	1.3	A, C	FEB	34
MAPCO.................	46¼	1.10	2.4	PC	JAN	17
Marriott.................	9⅝	Stock only	—	P	FEB	29
McDermott...............	53¾	1.60	3.0	P	FEB	13
McDonalds...............	42⅞	0.10	0.2	C	JAN	26
McDonnell Douglas........	20¾	0.50	2.4	PC	FEB	18
Merck...................	55⅜	1.50	2.7	C	JAN	19
Merrill Lynch.............	19½	0.80	4.1	A, C, PC	JAN	25
Mesa Petroleum..........	33¾	0.10	0.3	A	JAN	30
Minnesota Mining & Mfg...	51¾	1.70	3.3	C	JAN	16
Mobil Oil................	68½	3.80	5.6	C	FEB	14
Monsanto................	78¾	2.80	3.6	C	JAN	15
J. P. Morgan.............	50⅝	2.00	4.0	PC	JAN	12
Motorola................	46¼	0.84	1.8	A	JAN	15
NCR Corp...............	35¼	0.80	2.3	C	JAN	19
NL Industries............	21½	1.20	5.6	PC, P	FEB	20
National Distillers & Chemicals...............	25¾	1.60	6.2	A	FEB	12
National Semiconductor....	20¾	None	—	C, A	FEB	52
Northwest Airlines.........	25½	0.50	2.0	C	JAN	20
NW Industries............	54½	2.25	4.1	M	MAR	18
Norton Simon............	18¾	0.60	3.2	A	FEB	14

TABLE 3-1 (*continued*)

Underlying Stock	Price	Annual Dividend	Per-cent Yield	Exchanges Trading	Cycle	Percent Volatility
Occidental Petroleum	27¼	$1.00	3.7	C	FEB	34
Owens Illinois	27	1.06	3.9	M	MAR	12
PPG Industries	55¾	2.20	3.9	P	FEB	14
J. C. Penney	40¼	1.48	3.7	A	FEB	22
Pennzoil	32⅛	1.40	4.4	C	JAN	14
Pepsico	73⅞	2.40	3.2	C	JAN	12
Pfizer	28⅛	0.96	3.4	A	JAN	10
Phelps Dodge	34½	2.20	6.4	A	JAN	15
Philip Morris	55⅞	1.30	2.3	A	JAN	12
Philips Petroleum	58⅜	2.00	3.4	A	FEB	10
Pitney Bowes	19¾	0.80	4.1	A	JAN	18
Pittston	33⅜	1.25	3.7	P	FEB	18
Polaroid	34½	0.50	1.4	C, PC	JAN	17
Procter & Gamble	78½	2.60	3.3	A	JAN	14
RCA Corp	29⅞	1.20	4.0	C, PC	JAN	13
Ralston Purina	15¾	0.40	2.5	M	MAR	8
Raytheon	60	2.00	3.3	C	FEB	16
Reserve Oil & Gas	16⅜	0.20	1.2	A	FEB	37
Revlon	39⅞	0.90	2.3	M	MAR	11
Reynolds Ind	64½	3.28	5.1	C	FEB	12
Reynolds Metal	42¾	1.20	2.8	PC	FEB	12
Rite Aid Corp	15¾	0.24	1.5	A	JAN	16
Rockwell International	33¾	2.20	6.5	M	MAR	12
Safeway	46⅝	2.20	4.7	M	MAR	12
Sambo's	15⅝	0.48	3.1	PC	JAN	18
Santa Fe Int'l	49⅝	0.30	0.6	PC	JAN	38
Schering Plough	35	1.00	2.9	PC	FEB	26
Schlumberger	64¼	0.80	1.2	C	FEB	16
Scott Paper	17⅝	0.76	4.3	P	JAN	20
Seaboard Coast Line	38¼	2.00	5.2	P	JAN	20
Searle	12⅜	0.52	4.2	A	FEB	18
Sears Roebuck	58⅛	2.10	3.6	C	JAN	14
Simplicity Pattern	12	0.50	4.2	A	FEB	22
Skyline	15½	0.32	2.1	C	FEB	22
Southern Co	16⅝	1.46	8.8	C	FEB	12
Sperry Rand	34⅝	0.92	2.6	C	JAN	19
Standard Oil California	40	2.20	5.5	A	JAN	15
Standard Oil Indiana	54⅜	2.60	4.8	C	FEB	13
Sterling Drugs	14⅝	0.70	4.8	A	FEB	14
Sun Oil Co	44¾	2.00	4.5	P	FEB	24
Syntex	19¼	0.50	2.6	C	JAN	32
TRW, Inc	37⅜	1.40	3.7	A	JAN	12
Tandy	35	None	—	A, C	JAN	20
Teledyne	58	Stock only	—	C, P, PC	JAN	32
Tenneco	33	1.88	5.7	A	FEB	18
Tesoro	12¼	1.00	8.2	C	JAN	14
Texaco	26¾	2.00	7.5	A	JAN	10
Texas Instruments	85¾	1.32	1.5	C	JAN	24
Texas Gulf	28⅝	1.20	4.2	C	FEB	15
Tiger International	11½	0.50	4.3	A	FEB	26

TABLE 3–1 (*concluded*)

Underlying Stock	Price	Annual Dividend	Per-cent Yield	Exchanges Trading	Cycle	Percent Volatility
Transamerica.............	14	$0.66	4.7	P	FEB	21
Travelers.................	33	1.28	3.9	PC	FEB	16
UAL, Inc.................	21⅜	0.60	2.8	C	FEB	17
Union Carbide............	58¼	2.80	4.8	A	JAN	14
Union Oil Calif...........	53½	2.20	4.1	PC	JAN	17
Union Pacific.............	57⅛	1.70	3.0	P	FEB	14
US Steel.................	48½	2.20	4.5	A	JAN	13
United Technology........	37⅛	1.20	3.2	C	FEB	14
Upjohn..................	33⅝	1.08	3.2	C	JAN	16
Va. Elec. & Power.........	14⅝	1.24	8.5	P	JAN	14
Jim Walter...............	32¼	1.20	3.7	C	FEB	22
Warner Lambert..........	27⅜	1.00	3.7	A	JAN	14
Western Union...........	17½	1.40	8.0	P	JAN	10
Westinghouse.............	20	0.972	4.9	A	JAN	14
Weyer Haeuser...........	40⅞	0.80	2.0	C	JAN	12
Williams Cosmetics........	24⅛	1.00	4.1	C	FEB	14
Woolworth, F. W..........	25¾	1.40	5.4	P	FEB	14
Xerox...................	48¼	1.20	2.5	C, PC	JAN	18
Zenith Radio.............	24⅜	1.00	4.1	A	FEB	24

Data as of April 15, 1977.
Key:
    A = American Stock Exchange
    C = Chicago Board of Options Exchange
    M = Midwest Stock Exchange
    P = Philadelphia, Baltimore, Washington Exchange
    PC = Pacific Coast Exchange

average price were expected to be 50. A list of these volatility measures is presented in Table 3–1 along with dividend yields and the exchanges trading the options. The volatility for most stocks is a rather stable measure from year to year.

Where large changes in volatility do occur, they are usually associated with fundamental changes in a company's earnings outlook, or a major change in the general trend of stock prices. To play it safe, it is wise to compute a volatility from the most recent 52 weeks of price data, either from the *Media General Financial Weekly* or a long-term stock chart, such as R. W. Mansfield's weekly stock charts.[2]

How are the key variables that determine option premiums interrelated? The most renowned mathematical model solving this problem was developed by Fisher Black and Myron Scholes and published in the *Financial Analysts Journal* in July–August 1975. The value of a call premium is determined as follows:

$$\text{Value} = P_{\text{stock}}\, N(D_1) - P_{\text{exer}}\, N(D_2)e^{-R\Delta t}$$

where

$$D_1 = \frac{ln(P_{\text{stock}} \div P_{\text{exer}}) + (R + \tfrac{1}{2}V^2)\,\Delta t}{V\sqrt{\Delta t}}$$

$$D_2 = \frac{ln(P_{\text{stock}} \div P_{\text{exer}}) + (R - \tfrac{1}{2}V^2)\,\Delta t}{V\sqrt{\Delta t}}$$

$$N(D_1) = \frac{1}{\sqrt{2\pi}} \int_{-\infty}^{D1} e^{-\frac{1}{2}\,t2}\, dt$$

The variables are:

V = Volatility such as Malkiel's

$$\frac{\text{52-week high} - \text{52-week low}}{(\text{52-week high} + 52 \text{ week low})/2}$$

R = Short-term, riskless interest rate such as a 90-day T-Bill rate.

Δt = The time left in an option's life.

P stock = Current price of the underlying stock.

P exer = The exercise or strike price of the option.

---

[2] R. W. Mansfield & Co., 26 Journal Square, Jersey City, N.J., 07306.

The model was formulated by defining an arbitrage between selling the precise number of calls whose change in value over a small price change in the underlying stock equaled the change in value of the purchased stock itself. Since there is no risk in such an arbitrage, it is assumed that the strategy's return equals the rate on riskless short-term government debt instruments. The erosion in time premiums of the option sold, which accrue to the arbitrageur, provide this risk-free profit.

The Black-Scholes model has been programmed into the computers of most major brokerage firms. Fortunately, Texas Instruments has made the model available to users of their SR-52 programmable calculator.[3] Not only does the calculator compute a fair value call premium, but it also gives the neutral hedge ratio for the neutral call write-buy stock hedge defined by the model. This is a handy tool for serious options investors.

The early emphasis in tradeable options has obviously been on call premiums, but what about put premiums? How are they determined and what relationship do they have to call premiums? First of all, it should be remembered that supply and demand in the auction market determine the premiums paid for all options. The merchandise in greatest demand must be exchanged at the highest price. In the world of options, calls are the most popular item. This is so

---

[3] Texas Instruments, Inc., P.O. Box 5012, Dallas, Tex. 75222.

mainly because more investors own stocks for which call writing provides an added source of income. The analogous put strategy is to write puts and simply hold cash in preparation to purchase stock in case of a put exercise. Such an exercise would only occur if a stock has dropped below the exercise price. This results in owning a stock at a cost equal to the put strike price less the put premium collected. The alternate put writing approach is to short one hundred shares of an underlying stock combined with the writing of a put. The risk in this strategy is that if a sharp rally occurs, the put premium may possibly be kept without fear of exercise, but once the extent of the rally exceeds the put premium, the potential loss is only limited by how much further the stock can rally.

On top of all this, put premiums are less than call premiums, again due to lower demand, limiting the potential reward of pure put strategies. To further aggravate the situation, put-call arbitrage by major brokerage houses tends to depress put premiums and enhance call premiums. The process involved is called conversion. This term is derived from the process of converting a call to a put developed in the over-the-counter option market, which preceded the present auction market. Conversion was a response to the need of providing an adequate supply of calls. The conversion house would buy a put from the straddle writer, write a call and buy 100 shares of the underlying stock. This is a no-risk strategy because if the stock rose in price, the call would be exercised with the stock delivered out at the exercise price. The profit would be the call premium received less the cost of the put. A side benefit was the possibility that a put kept after a call exercise could also become profitable if a stock dropped in price. Or, the free put could be used as an insurance policy on the purchase of additional stock.

In today's world, the major brokerage houses use the auction market to short excess stock held in their cages as a way of generating cash from the short sale, which earns interest while they carry a riskless short put–long call hedged position. The long call is an insurance cost. The money earned on the short generated cash and the put premium provides the revenues. This arbitrage process is an added opportunity offered sophisticated brokerage firms to make greater use of their otherwise idle assets. Since the dollars involved are sizable, this is another supply-demand pressure in the market place which enhances call premiums while depressing put premiums.

There is even a formula to express this set of relationships. It is the well-known conversion formula developed for European style options which, unlike Clearing Corporation options, can only be exercised on their final day. The equation is as follows:

$$P = C - S + dD + \frac{E}{1 + nr}$$

where

> P = Put premium
> C = Call premium
> S = Stock price
> dD = The present value of dividends that would go ex during the life of the option
> E = Strike price
> n = Fraction of a year remaining until expiration
> r = Short-term interest rate expressed as a decimal (e.g., 6 percent would be .06)

For a call premium of 5, a stock price of 90, no dividends (for ease of computation), a strike price of 100, an option life of eight months, and a short-term interest rate of 6 percent, the put premium can be computed as follows:

$$P = 5 - 90 + dD + \frac{100}{1 + (8/12)(.06)}$$

$$= 5 - 90 + \frac{100}{1 + .04}$$

$$= 5 - 90 + 96.15 = 101.15 - 90 = 11.15$$

Thus an eight-month call, 10 points out of the money, which costs 5 ($500 for 100 shares of stock), is equivalent to a put 10 points in the money which costs 11.15. If the stock price were 100 and the call premium 10, the equivalent put premium would be 6.15, the difference being the eight months' worth of a 6-percent return on the $10,000 worth of stock sold short.

In order to provide the reader with an independent means of computing put and call premiums, a set of premium curves follows, which require a minimum of computation. As Figure

3–1 indicates, the graphs are a family of premium curves with S/E numbers above each line, where S is the stock price and E the exercise price. If the stock price were 110 and the exercise price 100, the S/E ratio would be 1.10. For a six-month-old option with an S/E ratio of 1.10, the correct call premium is found by entering the bottom of the graph at six months, moving up to the 1.10 line, then moving directly left to the answer of 20 percent. In dollar terms, this is 20 percent of the strike price of 100 or 20 ($2,000 for 100 shares).

The put premiums are found in the same manner, using the put premium graphs which follow the call premium graphs.

All premiums calculated by the preceding method assume no appreciable dividend yield for the underlying stock. To be more accurate in the case of high-yielding stocks—i.e., 3 percent and over—the premiums from the estimating graphs can be corrected by subtracting the appropriate yield for the time period involved from the graphical estimation. The suggested calculation would be:

$$\text{Premium adjustment} = -\frac{\text{Time to maturity}}{12 \text{ months}} \times \text{Annual yield}$$

For a stock yielding 6 percent and an option with three months to maturity, the correction would be:

$$\text{Premium adjustment} = \frac{-3 \text{ months}}{12 \text{ months}} \times 6\%$$
$$= -\frac{1}{4} \times 6\% = -1.5\%$$

In actuality, option premiums tend to adjust downward by this amount when a stocks goes ex-dividend, so that dividends are an important consideration when estimating a premium. Your stockbroker should be contacted to determine whether an intended purchase or sale is about to miss a dividend payment.

The reader is now equipped to properly evaluate option premiums. The next logical step is applying these skills to the proper selection and operation of option strategies. This is discussed in the next chapter.

FIGURE 3-1

Call Premiums during Their Life
(volatility—10 percent)

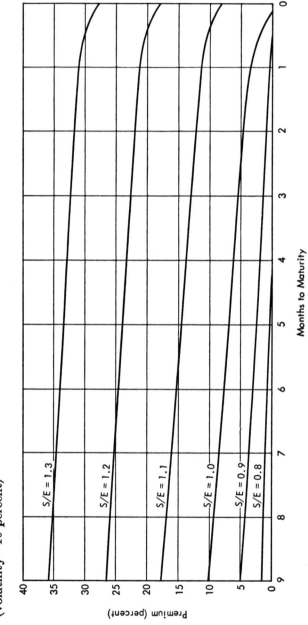

Note: S/E = Stock price divided by exercise price.

FIGURE 3-2
Call Premiums during Their Life
(volatility—20 percent)

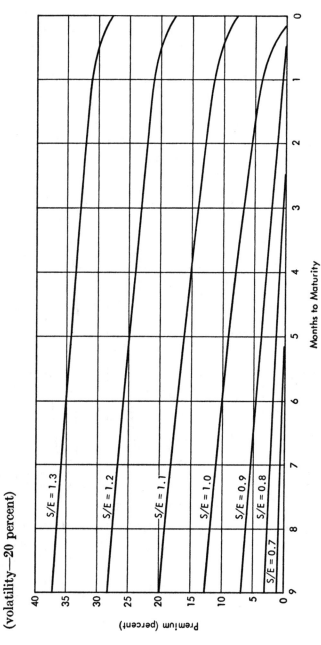

Note: S/E = Stock price divided by exercise price.

FIGURE 3-3
Call Premiums during Their Life
(volatility—30 percent)

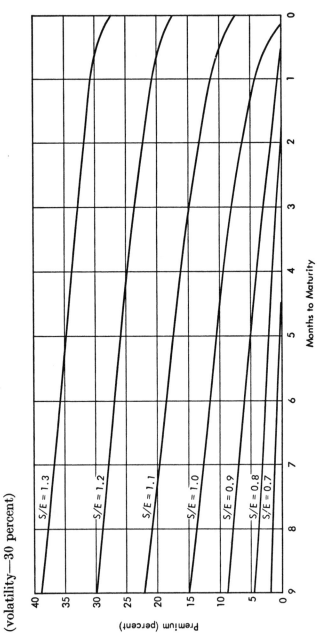

Note: S/E = Stock price divided by exercise price.

FIGURE 3-4

Call Premiums during Their Life
(volatility—40 percent)

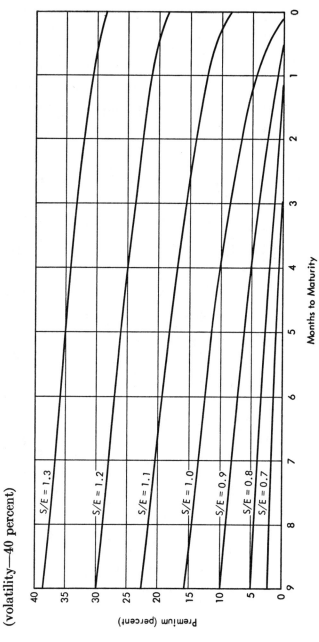

Note: S/E = Stock price divided by exercise price.

FIGURE 3-5

Call Premiums during Their Life

(volatility—50 percent)

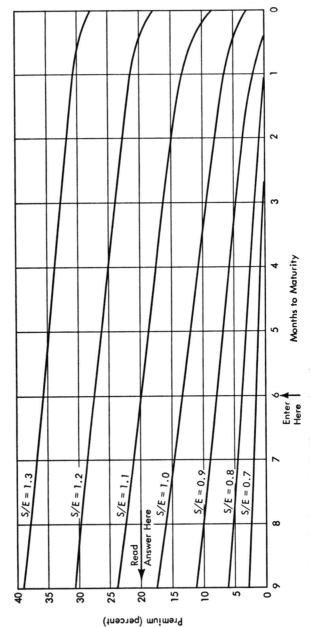

Note: S/E = Stock price divided by exercise price.

FIGURE 3–6

Put Premiums during Their Life

(volatility—10 percent)

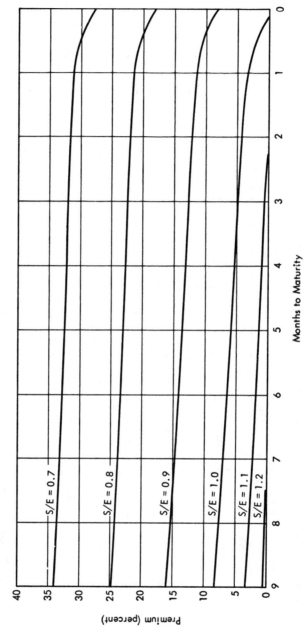

Note: S/E = Stock price divided by exercise price.

FIGURE 3-7
Put Premiums during Their Life
(volatility—20 percent)

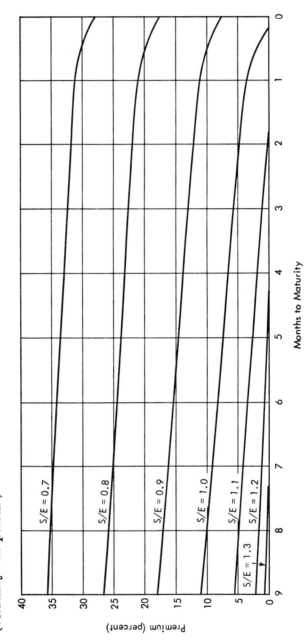

Note: S/E = Stock price divided by exercise price.

FIGURE 3-8

Put Premiums during Their Life

(volatility—30 percent)

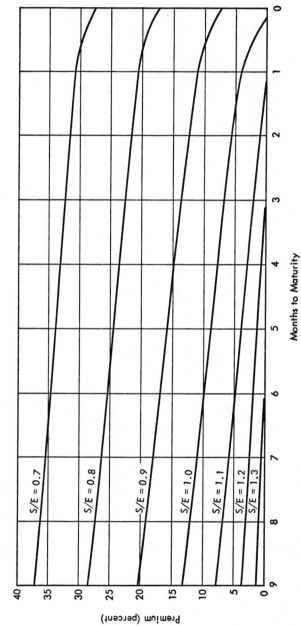

Note: S/E = Stock price divided by exercise price.

FIGURE 3-9

Put Premiums during Their Life

(volatility—40 percent)

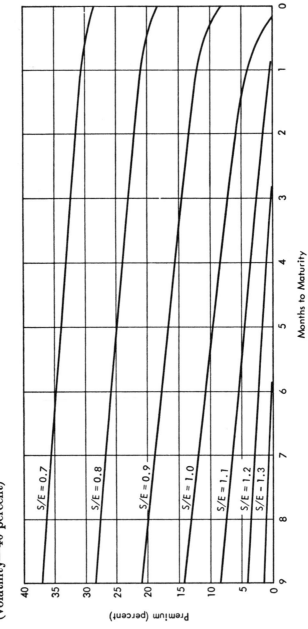

Note: S/E = Stock price divided by exercise price.

FIGURE 3-10

Put Premiums during Their Life

(volatility—50 percent)

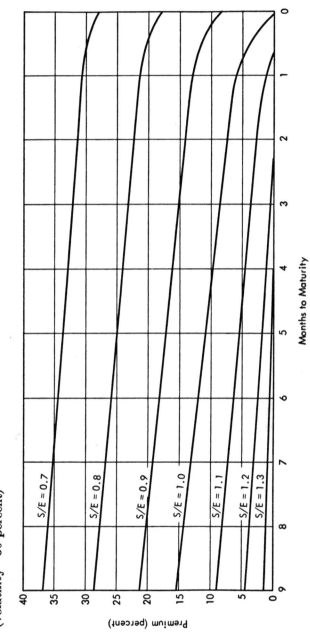

Months to Maturity

Note: S/E = Stock price divided by exercise price.

Setting Strategies

4

A ny option strategy applied rigidly for a long
enough period will result in the loss of all
capital. There is a correct strategy—or, in the
case of the CBOE, there are several correct strategies—for a given market environment. The key
is to define the environment and then match it
with the appropriate strategies.

But, before getting involved in environments,
what do we mean by a strategy? It is a set of
procedures designed to attain a desired goal,
which in this case is a profit on our invested
capital. The process can be thought of in terms
of a military campaign. We have reserves, our
capital, and we desire to employ them to achieve
a victory, a monetary profit. With great hopes
and little experience, the initial instinct is to
attack, to overwhelm the enemy with all our reserves. If we face a wise opponent, and the
marketplace draws the most brilliant talent in
the world, he lets us spend our reserves in one
false move and our war is lost. Or, if we are
more conservative, but unwise, we may fritter
away our reserves in one false move after another.

As we grow older and wiser and gain the experience of our own losses and those of others, we learn to develop a second skill, defense. This learning sequence is true in all contests, whether military, athletic, or otherwise. The college star spends his first years as a professional learning that the key to winning consistently is to have a good defense as well as an offense. This is the only successful approach when you face stiff competition. The veteran who wants to play for many years avoids the one total burst of energy by which he risks everything for the sake of glory. It is glamorous, it may make headlines, but it is usually characteristic of a short, meteoric career. The pro provides a good defense to avoid being hurt badly, and launches a wise offense to capitalize on the weakness of his opponents. When he sees an opportunity for victory, he may strike firmly, but never in such a manner that if he is wrong he is destroyed. This concept is of utmost importance in our case, since the most significant feature of stock options is their capability of providing a stock market defense. Defense in this sense is the minimizing of capital losses as we go about our business of making capital profits.

As we mentioned in the introduction to the CBOE, its aftermarket for options permits the application of strategies ranging from a heavy dependence on market timing and stock selection, all the way to strategies which lack forecasts and assume random-walk stock price behavior. Investigating this spectrum is probably the best means of introducing the major strategies covered in this book.

The most aggressive option strategies attempt to use a minimum of money to gain a profit usually in excess of 100 percent a year for the money involved in the trade, if it works. Invariably, if the potential rewards are great so is the risk of loss. Most beginning investors are blind to this fact, not so much because they can't see that the risk of loss exists, but rather that they don't want to see. When personal money is involved, especially when it is a large part of one's bankroll, it is virtually impossible to be objective. The major enemy in the battle for profits is your own emotions and, when money is at stake, the most deep-seated and powerful ones come into play. It is amazing to see how many people engage in high risk/high reward strategies without ever considering the risk. At the height of a bull market, the spinster school teacher who hears about fortunes being made in the stock market takes her lifetime savings of $5,000 and doesn't buy General Motors, but 1,000 shares of an over-the-counter stock in a company with no business, with inexperienced management, with merely the promise of a new product that will change the world. She has purchased a dream, the chance to make a fortune, and instead loses it all. Or, the hard-nosed business executive, about to retire, who gambles his lifetime fortune of $200,000 on a new venture so that he can have some big money to retire on. Both of these people, who are by no means unusual, forgot or didn't consider their defense. A high risk/high reward strategy is fine, as long as the odds favor success and a small amount of total capital is employed. When little is at stake, you can take a big gamble with equanimity. When everything is at stake you choke up and lose it all. It's as simple as that.

The major strategies available will be presented according to their respective risk/reward class. This is done so that the reader can begin to match his goals and suitability with the strategies which are correct for him. Suitability should be a major concern for the individual in the sense that he should match his pocketbook to his investing. When using the riskiest strategies he should be able to lose all his capital without cramping his life-style or affecting his ability to pay his bills. Likewise, he should not risk all his investing capital in the high risk area, but rather restrict it to a small portion such as less than 20 percent. The safer strategies will allow him to risk more of his investing capital. As each risk/reward area is covered the strategies for both bull and bear markets will be presented, so that the reader will begin to see many of the reciprocal relationships which exist between puts and calls. To avoid confusion a table, Table 4–1, is presented which sorts out the various strategies according to the proper market conditions for their application. It might be helpful to refer back to that table as each strategy is discussed in order to see how it fits in with the other strategies as well as with the condition of the market.

The most common high risk/high reward strategies using options are the purchases of puts or calls, or the writing of uncovered op-

TABLE 4-1
Table of Strategies

Nature of Strategy	Name of Strategy	Risk	Reward	Ideal Price Environment	Profit Potential if Successful	Strategy Characteristics
1. High risk/ high reward	Call buying	Loss of premium	Limited only by degree of stock price rise	Bull market	100–300%/year	Requires the maximum skill in stock selection and market timing
2. High risk/ high reward	Put buying	Loss of premium	Limited by drop of stock price to zero	Bear market	100–300%/year	Requires the maximum skill in stock selection and market timing
3. High risk/ high reward	Writing calls, naked	Limited only by degree of stock price rise	Limited to call premium	Bear market	50–100%/year	Requires good skill in stock selection and timing
4. High risk/ high reward	Writing puts, naked	Limited by drop of stock price to zero	Limited to put premium	Bull market	50–100%/year	Requires good skill in stock selection and timing
5. Moderate risk/ moderate reward	Buying stock, buying a put for protection	Limited to the cost of the put option	Limited only by rise in stock price, less the cost of the put	Bull market	25%/year with no margin	Requires good skill in stock selection and timing plus premium evaluation
6. Moderate risk/ moderate reward	Shorting stock, buying a call for protection	Limited to the cost of the call option	Limited only by the drop in the stock price to zero, less the cost of the call	Bear market	25%/year	Requires good skill in stock selection and timing plus premium evaluation
7. Moderate risk/ moderate reward	Writing calls, fully hedged	Stock drops to zero less premiums collected	Call premium + stock appreciation to strike price	Bull market	15–25%/year with no margin	Requires good skill in stock selection and timing plus premium evaluation
8. Moderate risk/ moderate reward	Writing puts, fully hedged	Limited only by how much stock can appreciate during option's life less premiums	Put premium + stock drop to strike price	Bear market	15–25%/year	Requires good skill in stock selection and timing plus premium evaluation

TABLE 4-1 (continued)

Nature of Strategy	Name of Strategy	Risk	Reward	Ideal Price Environment	Profit potential if Successful	Strategy Characteristics
9. Minimal risk/ moderate reward	Writing calls, partially hedged	Stock prices move beyond breakeven levels	Limited by call premiums & stock appreciation to strike prices	Bull or bear market	15–25%/year	Requires good market monitoring, decision-making, and premium evaluation skill
10. Minimal risk/ moderate reward	Writing puts, partially hedged	Stock prices move beyond breakeven levels	Limited by put premiums & stock drop to strike prices	Bear market	15–25%/year	Requires good market monitoring, decision-making, and premium evaluation skill
11. Minimal to no risk/moderate reward	Spreading	Difference between premium income and cost of purchased option plus difference in strike prices	Limited by amount of premiums written plus long option appreciation to strike price of options written	Bull or bear market	15–25%/year	Requires good market monitoring, decision-making, and premium evaluation skill
12. Minimal risk/ modest reward	Neutral hedge	Stock prices move beyond breakeven levels	Limited by call premiums + stock appreciation to strike prices	Bull or bear market	50% greater than the prime rate	Requires good market monitoring, decision-making, and premium evaluation skill

tions. A call is purchased to participate in an increase in price of the underlying stock. The advantages over buying the stock itself are that less money is required to purchase the option, while the option usually changes in value in proportion with the underlying stock. Therefore a small initial investment can yield a far larger percentage return than a simple stock purchase. For an OTC call the value of the call changes one for one with the underlying stock, but there is virtually no market to resell the call unless the change in stock price has been greater than the premium paid for the call. The same comparison can be made with a put option, only in this case the put buyer expects to profit from a drop in the underlying stock's price.

For the CBOE call options, the change in option value can be far from a one-to-one change with the stock price change if the option is well "out of the money" (as we shall see later in the book) and only approaches a one-to-one price change if the option is well "in the money." This also holds true for CBOE put options. The potential reward in all cases of buying options depends on the amount of price move that the underlying stock can experience during the life of the option. The option buyer is essentially purchasing a slice of time during which he expects a large stock price move to occur. Most option buyers don't understand this and rarely "cash in" their profit if a large price move occurs early in the option's life. The usual reasoning (call it greed) is that "if I made 200 percent on my money in one month, just think

of how much I can make in six months." The
investor fails to realize that such a price move
occurs for one stock in a thousand, even in the
best of bull markets. The risk side of the transaction is that the entire premium paid for the
option can be lost. As long as a fraction of investing capital has been committed to such a venture, the investor can at least survive to play
another day. The other high risk/high reward
option strategy is uncovered writing. The tactic
in this case is to write an option without owning
the stock to guarantee the option in the case of
a call, or without desiring to purchase the stock
to honor a put. This strategy is essentially a
gamble that the stock price in question will move
in a forecast direction during the life of the option. In the case of writing uncovered calls the
writer is speculating that the stock price will
remain unchanged (if the strike price equals
the current stock price)[1] or drop so that the
call will be unexercised, allowing the writer to
keep the premium he initially received when
the call was written. In the case of writing puts,
the writer speculates that the stock will remain
unchanged (if the strike price equals the current stock price)[1] or rise so that the option will
be unexercised and the premium retained by
the writer. While the option buyer's risk is
limited to the premium he paid and his reward
is bounded only by the degree of change in the

---

[1] This may seem a minor technicality, but it is possible
to write a CBOE option with a strike price below the
current market price which requires that the stock price
drops to or below the strike price to avoid an exercise.
Writing a put is the converse.

underlying stock, the reverse is true for the
naked writer. His reward is limited to the option premium, and yet his risk is only limited by
the amount the stock can move against him,
cushioned by the premium he collects. When
writing puts his risk is that the stock price will
drop from the strike price to zero less the
premium he collects. When writing calls, the
limit is how high the stock can rise above the
strike price during the option's life, again cushioned by the premium income.

One might superficially conclude that buying
options is far superior to writing naked because
of the opposite risk/reward characteristics. This
brings us back to the environment and the probabilities for success. In a bear market when most
stocks are dropping in price, 80 percent to 90
percent of calls may go unexercised.[2] If an investor has a capacity for identifying stocks in
trouble and times his call writing to coincide
with rally peaks he can be extremely successful.
And, with the CBOE, if he is wrong he can at
least buy back his calls to close out his obligation and achieve an ordinary loss. Since writing
puts is the opposite of writing calls, it makes
sense that writing puts would not be an ideal
bear market strategy. At the same token, buying
puts can be an excellent alternative to shorting
stocks in a bear market. There is more stress
on timing and stock selection than in writing
calls, but this is only because a stock has to drop
to give a put buyer a profit. A CBOE call writer

---

[2] "Near-Total Wipe-Out," *Barron's*, August 5, 1974.

can make a profit if the stock remains unchanged, drops in price, or even moves up slightly, as long as the erosion in time value for the call overtakes the stock price gain. The major difference is that naked-call writing offers better odds of earning a good return in a bear market with good consistency, while buying puts can offer spectacular profits, such as 200 percent to 300 percent in a month when the buyer is correct, but it is unusual to produce such results consistently. The same can be said about the comparison between writing puts and buying calls in a bull market.

The next layer of strategies can be categorized as moderate risk, moderate reward. The benchmark is a pretax profit of 20 percent to 40 percent pretax on invested capital. The writing of calls fully hedged or the shorting of stock matched with the purchase of an equal number of puts would fall in this class. Writing calls fully hedged means that an investor buys or owns the same amount of a given underlying stock that he has written call options for. The hoped for result is that the stock will rise in price so that the call is exercised. The call writer then retains the call premium, any stock dividends declared during the period for CBOE calls, plus the difference between the purchase price of the stock and the price the stock was delivered at to honor the call. If the writer is wrong and the stock declines, the CBOE writer can either close out his position to avoid any further loss, or simply collect the call premium as a cushion against the loss in his stock. Since the emphasis is on making money on a rising stock price, this is clearly a bull market strategy.

The bear market analog to writing calls fully hedged is obviously writing puts and shorting stock on a one for one basis. The emphasis is on making profits by collecting the put premiums, while the short stock provides the guarantee for the option contract. Since writing a put places the writer in a position of having to purchase 100 shares of stock at the option's strike price if the stock declines, the writer stands to profit if the stock remains unchanged or drops. In this case he collects the premium received during the option's life. Since he guarantees to purchase 100 shares of stock at the strike price, if he has shorted the stock at the same level he ends up essentially covering his short when the put is exercised at the same price he went short. He incurs commission costs in the process, but otherwise breaks even on his short stock. If the stock rose in price instead, the writer could withstand a gain up to the amount of premiums he received without suffering a loss. Beyond that point he would face a loss of $100 for every point the underlying stock rose beyond the amount of the put premium. On the profit side, the writer is limited to making a maximum profit of the premium less any dividends on the underlying stock. An investor who simply shorted a stock that dropped sharply in price could make more money, but again the questions of consistency and defense arise. The covered put writer has both in his favor in a bear market, whereas the unprotected shorting of stock runs the frequent risk of encountering a short squeeze plus loss of sleep.

A variation of covered writing is the purchasing of options as a hedge against a damaging move either with a stock purchase or short sale of stock. The emphasis in this case is on making a profit on a change in the stock price either up or down, with the purchase of a call providing short sale protection against a short squeeze and a put purchase hedging the buyer of stock against a severe drop in the stock's price. In each case the potential profit is diminished by the cost of the option, but so is the loss.

The next layer of risk/reward, in this case minimal risk/moderate reward, involves a variation of the fully hedged writing strategy just discussed. The variation is termed the partial hedge and consists of writing more options than shares of stock purchased to guarantee a call, or shorted to guarantee a put. This strategy demands a separate chapter ("The Moderate Reward/Minimal Risk Strategies"), but the essentials will be covered here.

The main feature of the partial hedge is the establishment of adjustable breakeven levels above *and* below the current price of the stock involved. This contrasts with the fully hedged strategy which has fixed breakeven levels and where the protective emphasis is on the downside. The partial hedge's double-sided protection is provided on the downside, in the case of call writing, by the call premiums derived from writing. On the upside, the protection is provided by the fact that the gain in the price of the underlying stock plus the premiums collected offset the loss incurred on having to purchase stock at the current market to guarantee the uncovered calls of the partial hedge. The effectiveness of this strategy lies in the ability to predetermine before establishing the position exactly what breakeven levels seem appropriate for a particular underlying stock. While this is often based on experience, on the degree of volatility inherent in a stock, and on measures of past price ranges over time, some practitioners employ sophisticated probability models to calculate the likelihood of a given breakeven level's being penetrated. The existence of the CBOE aftermarket makes this strategy especially attractive because of the ability to adjust the partial hedge during its life. If more upside protection is desired, this can be provided by reducing the net short position, either by purchasing more stock or by entering closing transactions for some of the calls. If greater downside protection is desired, this can be provided by writing more calls to generate more premiums relative to the stock held, or some stock can be sold in order to provide more premium protection per share of stock held.

While all the prior strategies mentioned are most successful either in a bull or a bear market, or are heavily dependent on the timing of purchases or sales, the partial hedge only requires that too large an upward or downward bias in the breakeven levels be avoided, especially at market turning points. (Determining the proper ratio of calls to stock is covered in the partial hedge chapter, but an extreme stance would be 20 calls short and 100 shares of stock long.)

The most balanced hedging approach assumes an initial neutral position (with regard to changes in the market value of the hedge) which can easily be adjusted as the underlying stock price changes.

An important criterion for successful partial hedging when writing calls is that premiums are large enough to provide a good degree of downside protection without having to write too many calls relative to the stock owned. If this becomes a severe problem, the sister strategy, writing puts and shorting stock can be substituted. Another substitute strategy, which lacks a great deal of the same flexibility, can be employed, namely, purchasing calls and shorting stock. In this case the inexpensive calls are purchased to capitalize on a hoped-for rise in the underlying stock's price, while the shorted stock provides a hedge in case the stock doesn't rally and the calls drop in value or possibly lose their value altogether. This is really a poor substitute for the partial hedge because it depends heavily on a price forecast for success, while the partial hedge minimizes the need for a forecast and provides far more latitude in making a profit.

A much purer substitute for the partial hedge is a technique called *spreading*, which essentially substitutes the purchase of calls in the place of buying stock as in a partial hedge. Spreading consists of selling calls for a given strike price and expiration date, while simultaneously purchasing calls in the same underlying stock, but usually for a different strike price and possibly even a different expiration date. The usual procedure is to write two or three calls for a particular strike price and expiration date coupled with the purchase of a call for a lower strike price (usually near the current market price of the underlying stock) and the same expiration date. If this is done properly the premiums generated by the written calls more than offset the cost of the purchased call. In this manner if the stock drops in price the premiums from the written calls are kept, offsetting the loss in the purchased call, which has become worthless. With this approach the strategy has no downside risk. On the other hand, if the underlying stock price increases, the purchased call will increase in value, while the value of the written calls also increases. The maximum amount of money is made if, at expiration day, the underlying stock price is at the strike price of the written calls. At this point the premiums are kept and a profit has been made on the purchased call. If the stock had risen above the upper strike price level, a point would be reached at which the loss in the written calls would overcome the call premiums plus the profit on the purchased call. This is obviously the upper breakeven level. The attractiveness of this strategy is that less capital is required than for the partial hedge plus the fact that the spread can be established so that there is no downside risk. The one major problem is that a modest pocketbook may get in trouble if too many large price rises occur because margin requirements for the written calls increase as the stock price rises and the positions may have to be involuntarily unwound. The offset is that this trouble will occur in the vicinity of greatest profit so that the unwinding due to margin restrictions often proves to be a blessing in disguise. As with the partial hedge, the only price forecast required is that of a likely price range during the holding period of the options.

We are now at the other end of the spectrum, the random walk approach to making a profit with options. The strategy is termed the neutral hedge. This technique is basically an arbitrage between the degree of change in the value of the calls written and the price change in the stock purchased as the other side of the arbitrage. At a particular point in the option's life and for a particular strike price and underlying stock price there is a normative degree of change between the call premiums and the price of the underlying stock over a small range of several points. A particular set of conditions might produce a $\frac{1}{4}$ point rise in the option premiums for every point rise in the stock price. In this case a neutral position would be four calls short, 100 shares of stock long. For any minor changes around this level as much money will be lost on the short calls as is gained with the stock, as well as the reverse. If the stock moved to a higher price level, the ratio of call premium change to stock price change might be 1 to 2. In this case the position would be adjusted to approximate the new ratio, either by closing out two short calls or purchasing another 100 shares of stock.

How is money made with this process? In two ways, through the deflation of an inflated call premium, which occurs usually because of temporary market conditions, and through the loss of the time value of the call as time passes, both of which accrue to the call writer. The key requirements for success with this "know nothing" approach is an ability to evaluate whether a call premium is above a normative level and therefore will decline in value over time, and a monitoring system to flag such situations. In addition, an excellent trading capability is required to capitalize on these situations as they occur.

One caveat must be mentioned regarding the operation of any of the above mentioned arbitrage strategies. A United States taxpayer must always bear in mind that if a stock drops in price he may be faced with the unfavorable tax consequence of a capital loss, which is difficult to write off, and ordinary income, which can be taxed at a very high rate.

This broad brush coverage of a range of strategies should provide an overview of the most likely methods of managing money to be encountered if one uses options. It should serve as an introduction to the detailed treatment of the strategies which will follow and will include specific rules for establishing and closing positions, capital management, and the personal skill required to successfully engage in each of the strategies. Before going on, however, it might be helpful to review Table 4–1, which summarizes the characteristics of the various strategies.

It can easily be seen that the existence of a

bull or bear market determines the success or failure of many of the strategies, while timing and stock selection are a determinant of success for the high risk/high reward strategies. For these reasons, the next logical subject of investigation is price behavior.

Price Behavior

5

The paradox of Wall Street is that price, the determinant of stock market profits, is the least understood variable in investing. And while certain option strategies depend far less on an accurate price forecast than simply dealing in stocks alone, the need still exists to understand the price action of the underlying stock.

Price is said to be determined by fundamental, technical, and psychological factors, but most fundamentalists have a horrible record of forecasting future price directions, the typical Wall Street technicians have been disgraced by their lack of counter evidence to the random walk theorists who say that future stock prices can't be predicted, and no one seems to have organized market psychology into any measurable fashion. Where does that leave us?

Perhaps we can begin by asking how much money we can expect to make annually on the long side if we could forecast prices with any degree of accuracy. To accomplish this, let's review the behavior of the stock market for the past 25 years. Assuming we have perfect hindsight and can purchase a portfolio of blue chip stocks called the Dow Jones Industrial Average at the lowest point each year and sell at the highest price later that year, what would our average annual gain be? The number is a surprisingly low 21.2 percent annually, considering how accurate we have to be to achieve that level. As Table 5–1 indicates, if it were not for three extraordinary years, 1954, 1958, and 1970, the overall average would have been 18.6 percent.

TABLE 5–1

25 Years of Market History: Picking the Exact Low and Best Succeeding High Each Year

	Low	High	Percent Change
1949	160.6	201	25.2
1950	192	237	23.4
1951	234	277	18.4
1952	256	293	14.5
1953	254.4	285	12.0
1954	279	408	46.2*
1955	384	491	27.9
1956	459	525	14.4
1957	453	523	15.5
1958	429	591	37.8*
1959	571	684	19.8
1960	596	663	11.2
1961	607	742	22.2
1962	525	659	25.5
1963	643	773	24.2
1964	755	898	18.9
1965	832	976	17.3
1966	735	828	12.7
1967	776	952	22.7
1968	817	994	21.7
1969	789	871	10.4
1970	627	849	35.4*
1971	826	958	16.0
1972	882	1042	18.1
1973	845	997	18.0
25 Year Average.			21.2

* Average is 18.6 percent without three top years.

Of course, these averages do not include dividends, which have averaged roughly 3.5 percent during this period. With dividends included the total return would be 24.7 percent per year for the full 25 years. At the other end of the spectrum, Professor Eugene Fama of the University of Chicago has estimated a 9 percent average total return by purchasing stocks in 1929 and holding them through 1965. Considering these two extremes, the potential profit of 20 to 25 percent for the safe partial hedge strategy discussed in Chapter 4 appears rather attractive. At least the profit potential of the more conservative option strategies should be placed in better perspective. The truth is that any equity money manager in the early 1970s would gladly accept even the 9 percent result.

What can we say about price behavior? Is it truly random as the random walk theorists propose? Or is there some order in the price madness? One phenomenon that seems to occur with a high degree of regularity is the major selling climax that has ended every major bear market for the past 25 years. (Some analysts have supposedly taken the cycle back much farther.) If one uses as a measure of selling climaxes the percent of New York Stock Exchange issues making a low in a given week the pattern is rather striking, as the graph in Figure 5–1 indicates. Except for several weeks in 1969, the minus 50 percent level has been exceeded only once every 50 months. As Table 5–3 indicates, a range of 45.7 to 55.3 months contains 90 percent of the variation about the 50-month cycle

FIGURE 5–1

The Regularity of Major Selling Climaxes

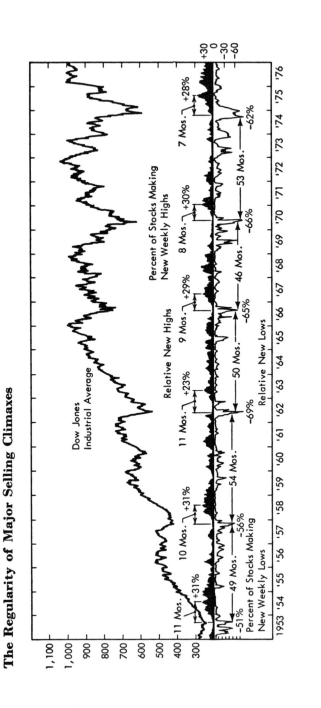

TABLE 5–2

Selling Climax Month	Time to Next Climax (months)	Time from Selling Climax to Peak New Highs
June, 1949...............	51	7 months to January, 1950
Sept. 1953...............	49	10 months to August, 1954
Oct. 1957...............	54	9 months to August, 1958
June, 1962...............	50	11 months to May, 1963
Aug. 1966...............	46	9 months to May, 1967
June, 1970...............	53	8 months to January, 1971
October, 1974............		7 months to May, 1975

TABLE 5–3

Time between Climaxes

Mean............................	50.5 months
Standard Deviation.................	2.9 months
Range...........................	46 to 54 months
90% Confidence Limits	
Mean − 1.65 Sigma = ...	45.7 months
Mean + 1.65 Sigma = ...	55.3 months

TABLE 5-4

Time from Climax to Peak New Highs

Mean............................	8.7 months
Standard deviation..................	1.5 months
Range...........................	7 to 11 months
90% Confidence Limits	
Mean − 1.65 Sigma = ...	6.2 months
Mean + 1.65 Sigma = ...	11.2 months

mean. Perhaps even more amazing is the fact that, the majority of the time, the peak percent of new highs made in a bull market occurs from seven to 11 months after a selling climax low. This is probably the most striking example of regularity in stock prices.

What about the random walk theory? Is it valid or is it not? To answer such questions one should first define what we mean by a random walk. The term comes from a model of molecular behavior that describes something called brownian motion, or the fact that the molecules of a gas do not move in any well-defined path. The name random walk comes from the mathematics which describes such random molecular motion by assuming, as with a drunk, that a step in a particular direction offers no predictability of the direction of any future steps. The stock market analogy of the model tested whether a price movement on a given day had any relationship with the price movement at some fixed time in the future, whether one day later, 30 days or longer. The results of such studies[1] convincingly indicate that such a measure of price behavior does not show any link between the present and the future. This was a major contribution. The results convincingly proved that anyone who thought he saw a price pattern today which could predict with any degree of reliability a price pattern in the future was kidding himself. Experienced Wall Street money managers knew long before the random walkers that standard technical analysis yielded random results.

Where the random walk theorists seem to have gone awry is with the conclusions they have

---

[1] Paul H. Cootner, ed., *The Random Character' of Stock Prices* (Cambridge, Mass.: MIT Press, 1967).

drawn from their research. The major one is that the stock market is a perfect market in the sense that all news developments are reflected instantaneously so that, again, there is no predictability in the news events. Such a conclusion not only lacks common sense, but leads to the ridiculous logic that, since the market is perfect, security analysis is a wasted effort. But without security analysts' processing the news inputs, the market would become imperfect, creating the need for security analysts because now there would be an imperfect market to take advantage of.

The common sense of the marketplace is that it is made up of people and there is a wide disparity between the abilities of these people to make money in the stock market. There are also wide discrepancies in the ability of market participants to perceive and understand the events that offer clues to future business conditions. And there is one correlation no scientist can deny, that of the long-run relationship between the level of profits and stock prices. All that the random walker can say is that a price wiggle today cannot predict a price wiggle either tomorrow or any other day. But that does not make the market.

There are a few successful stock market investors and they have one trait in common. They understand how the market crowd behaves and do the opposite. When the crowd has gotten excited about the future direction of stock prices and has moved them up, the professional sells. When the crowd is gripped with the fear that the world is coming to an end even though it isn't, the professional buys. He has learned by hard-earned experience that a price movement has stopped going up and all the money is spent when there is near universal agreement about how wonderful a situation is. A price can't go any higher unless there is a new buyer to enter the scene to pay up for the merchandise. If all passengers are on the train, the upward movement has to stop. The reverse is true when pessimism sets in. The price will drop until everyone who is disturbed by the fearsome developments has sold his stock. The price can go lower only as long as someone wants to sell some more stock. When all the scared sellers have sold, the price has to stop going down.

There is another curious phenomenon in the stock market and that has to do with how most people place their orders. It might seem logical that when someone wanted to act they would simply enter an order to either buy or sell a stock at the existing price. It seldom happens in this manner. A buyer seems to think of a stock as a piece of merchandise and if it has recently been selling at a slightly lower price, will attempt to place a limit order to own the stock at that price. Invariably, this is a mistake if the stock is heading higher in price. If so, the limit order will never be executed and the buyer will have missed his opportunity. If he does end up buying the stock because weakness has allowed the order to be filled, the stock usually heads lower and the investor ultimately finds that the purchase was a mistake.

Selling is a different story. This is the toughest decision to make because if the stock goes higher after it is sold, the investor feels he has made a mistake. If it later goes lower, he feels good. What does he do? He tries for the best of all worlds by putting in a sell order above the current price. His original desire to sell probably came from some recent sluggishness in the stock's price and his initial fears of a stock topping out were probably the best hunch. If the stock is entering a decline, his sell order will go unexecuted and he will have the worst of both worlds. The lesson is, don't try to let the price action make the decision for you through a limit order. If you want to own a stock, buy it at the current price. If you want to sell it, do the same. Price behavior, as this chapter demonstrates, is involved enough to be a subject unto itself.

How can someone understand this process? No mathematician ever will, unless he leaves his equations behind and lives in the marketplace. The understanding comes from experiencing your own emotions as you attempt to make money in the stock market. By doing this and observing the emotions of others who are attempting to do the same thing, you will find yourself wanting the comfort of buying into a well-established price move because you feel safe. At first, you will buy at the end of every up move, because you have a lot of company. You have joined the train with the last passengers to get on board. When the price begins to drop you first become discouraged, then nauseated, and then vomit the stock, right at the point it stops going down. If you are determined to succeed, you will keep trying, keep making mistakes, and then begin to realize why you have been wrong with almost 100-percent consistency. You *followed* the price behavior. Slowly you begin to see that you have to play outside of yourself. You have to let prices drop to the point that all the other price followers have sold. Then you buy. And when all the price followers have bought, you sell. You observe the other market participants around you who habitually buy at a top or sell at a bottom. Their behavior confirms your judgment. Any experienced broker can name at least ten of his customers who consistently buy at tops or sell at bottoms. People are the best measure of the market's position. Their nonrandomness would send a random walker back to his drawing board in a flash.

What is the answer? Does everyone have to leave his job and get involved full time in the market? Definitely not! The balance of this chapter will demonstrate some nonrandom price measuring tools that should offer some help to the part-time investor. Or, he will at least be able to realize his limitations.

In the chapter on setting strategies, Chapter 4, we mentioned the word *environment.* What we meant mainly was the price environment and, for want of a better term, used the terms *bull market* and *bear market.* In simplest terms a bull market is one in which the greatest percentage of stocks are experiencing a price progression of higher peaks and troughs with at least ten weeks between consecutive troughs or peaks. This is known as a stock with a major uptrend. If the successive peaks and troughs with a similar time period between them were moving to lower price levels, this would be a major downtrend stock and a market dominated by such stocks would be a Bear Market. Examples of both situations are presented in Figure 5–2. But what about a market dominated by neither uptrends nor downtrends? Logically it at least should have the possibility of existing. For the past ten years it has shown up for a period of several months, but quickly disappeared as the bull or bear market that had been in force prior to the period either resumed or changed to the opposite phase. It is important to be aware that such a market can exist because the short choppy price moves that dominate that kind of a market can wreak havoc on certain option strategies that are devastated by such short price swings (termed "whipsaws" in Wall Street parlance). Which leads to the question, How do we know what kind of a market we are in?

The commonsense way to define the current price environment seems to be simply to measure the composition of the market in terms of the percentage of stocks exhibiting strong uptrends as we define them, strong downtrends, or the residual of stocks going nowhere in particular. With a cutoff rate in appreciation or deterioration of 10 percent per annum, a 25-year study was conducted of the 100 largest market capitalization stocks on the New York Stock Exchange; the sample was broken into strong uptrend, strong downtrend, or an "others" category

FIGURE 5–2

A. Uptrend Stock

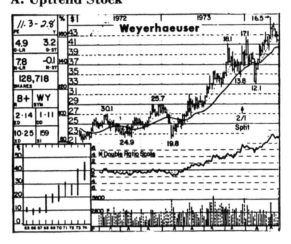

B. Downtrend Stock

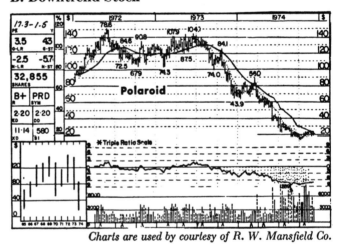

Charts are used by courtesy of R. W. Mansfield Co.

on a monthly basis and the percent composition of each segment was computed. The graph in Figure 5–3 is the result. Some very striking results become immediately apparent. Whenever more than 40 percent of the sample is exhibiting uptrend behavior, the Dow Jones Industrial Av-

FIGURE 5-3

The Market Barometer

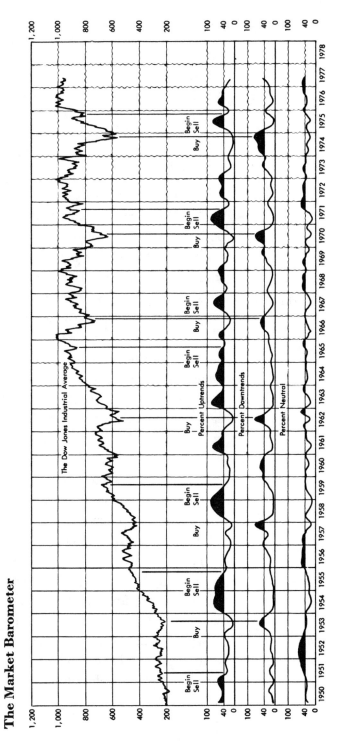

erage plotted at the top of the graph is in an uptrend. And whenever the Dow Jones Industrial Average is exhibiting downtrend behavior, the percent of stocks in significant downtrends is more than 40 percent. At key turning points, whether up or down, the residual measure is more than 40 percent of the total. So here, in very simple terms, we seem to have a tool for monitoring where we are. It doesn't say, "the bull market is headed for 1,000 in three months," but it tells us that, until proven otherwise, a bull market is in force and we should stress those strategies which favor such a market rather than attempt to accomplish something that the price environment does not favor. In addition, the quality of the bull market can be monitored in terms of the percent of uptrends because, in almost all cases, the peak level will be reached before the market top is made. This can warn of an impending change in direction or at least that it is becoming more difficult to make profits based on bull market strategies. Perhaps more importantly, the residual measure (percent neutral trends) can warn when price moves will be small and of short duration so that money is not committed to strategies depending on large price moves. For this reason perhaps the best title for this set of measures is "the market barometer," because it tells you the current price weather.

What has the barometer's record been? If one simply gauges the market based on the dominance of uptrends, downtrends, or trendless behavior, Table 5–5 details the change in the Dow Jones Industrial Average during these various

TABLE 5–5

The Stock Market's Trend Characteristics versus the Dow Jones Industrial Average

Market Dominated by	From	To	Dow Jones Industrial Average		
			Beginning of Period	End of Period	Percent Change
Uptrends..........	January 2, 1950 (17 months)	May 31, 1951	201.1	248.5	+23.6
Trendless......... (Positive bias)	May 31, 1951 (23 months)	April 30, 1953	245.5	275.0	+10.7
Downtrends........	April 30, 1953 (8 months)	December 31, 1953	275.0	280.5	+ 2.0
Uptrends..........	December 31, 1953 (21 months)	September 30, 1955	280.5	466.5	+66.3
Trendless......... (Positive bias)	September 30, 1955 (11 months)	August 31, 1956	466.5	502.0	+ 7.6
Trendless......... (Negative bias)	August 31, 1956 (12 months)	August 31, 1957	502.0	484.5	− 3.5
Downtrends........	August 31, 1957 (6 months)	February 28, 1958	484.5	439.7	− 9.2
Uptrends..........	February 28, 1958 (18 months)	August 31, 1959	439.7	664.0	+51.0
Trendless.........	August 31, 1959 (2 months)	October 31, 1959	664.0	647.5	− 2.5
Downtrends........	October 31, 1959 (14 months)	December 31, 1960	647.5	615.5	− 4.9

TABLE 5-5 (continued)

Market Dominated by	From	To	Dow Jones Industrial Average		
			Beginning of Period	End of Period	Percent Change
Uptrends..........	December 31, 1960 (13 months)	January 31, 1962	615.5	707.5	+14.9
Trendless.........	January 31, 1962 (3 months)	April 30, 1962	707.5	672.5	− 4.9
Downtrends.......	April 30, 1962 (5 months)	September 30, 1962	672.5	578.5	−14.0
Trendless.........	September 30, 1962 (3 months)	December 31, 1962	578.5	651.5	+12.6
Uptrends..........	December 31, 1962 (32 months)	August 31, 1965	651.5	895.5	+37.5
Trendless......... (Positive bias)	August 31, 1965 (3 months)	November 30, 1965	895.5	949.0	+ 6.0
Uptrends..........	November 30, 1965 (6 months)	May 31, 1966	949.0	897.0	− 5.5
Downtrends.......	May 31, 1966 (8 months)	January 31, 1967	897.0	844.0	− 5.9
Trendless.........	January 31, 1967 (2 months)	March 31, 1967	844.0	866.0	+ 2.6
Uptrends..........	March 31, 1967 (9 months)	December 31, 1967	866.0	897.0	+ 3.6
Trendless......... (Positive bias)	December 31, 1967 (6 months)	June 30, 1968	897.0	898.0	+ 0.1

Uptrends........	June 30, 1968 (9 months)	March 31, 1969	898.0	958.0	+ 6.7
Trendless........	March 31, 1969 (4 months)	July 31, 1969	958.0	825.5	–13.8
Downtrends......	July 31, 1969 (14 months)	September 30, 1970	825.5	767.0	– 7.1
Uptrends........	September 30, 1970 (11 months)	August 31, 1971	767.0	909.0	+18.5
Trendless........ (Positive bias)	August 31, 1971 (7 months)	March 31, 1972	909.0	941.0	+ 3.5
Uptrends........	March 31, 1972 (12 months)	March 31, 1973	941.0	951.0	+ 1.7
Trendless........ (Negative bias)	March 31, 1973 (4 months)	July 31, 1973	951.0	937.0	– 1.5
Downtrends......	July 31, 1973 (19 months)	February 28, 1975	937.0	739.5	–21.1
Uptrends........	February 28, 1975 (8 months)	October 31, 1975	739.5	837.0	+13.2
Trendless........	October 31, 1975 (4 months)	February 29, 1976	837.0	972.0	+16.1
Uptrends........	February 29, 1976 (7 months)	September 30, 1976	972.0	990.1	+ 1.9
Trendless........	October 1, 1976 (7 months)	April 30, 1977	990.1	927.0	– 6.4
Downtrends......	May 1, 1977	Present			

TABLE 5–6

The Barometer's Effectiveness

Average Gain in Uptrend Markets	*Average Loss in Downtrend Markets*	*Average Change in Trendless Markets*
+19.4%	−8.6%	+1.9%
Occurrences + in 11 of 12 cases	*Occurrences* − in 6 of 7 cases	*Occurrences* + in 8 cases − in 6 cases

periods. The results have been a 19.4 percent average gain in uptrend markets with a positive price change in 11 out of 12 cases. The average loss in downtrend markets is 8.6 percent with 6 out of 7 cases offering a negative result. For trendless markets, the average change was a gain of 1.9 percent with positive changes in 8 of the 14 cases. The record shown in Table 5–6, seems to demonstrate an ability to define the market's price bias.

But several other important results have been obtained. The periods of serious downtrend behavior as demonstrated by more than 40 percent of stocks in downtrends have helped to identify major market bottoms. If one uses the rule of fewer than 15-percent uptrends combined with more than 50-percent downtrends to define serious weakness, the first month's improvement after such negative readings has identified every major market bottom since 1950 within two months. If one purchased the Dow Jones Industrials at such a point and held until the first time the percent uptrend reading dropped back below 40 percent, the average gain would have

TABLE 5–7

Strategy: Purchase after Market Bottom, Sell when Percent Uptrends Return below 40 Percent

Major Bottom	Percent Uptrends Back below 40 Percent	Dow Jones Industrial Average at: Buy Signal	Sell Signal	Percent Change
August 31, 1953.....	October 31, 1955	262.0	455.0	+73.7 in 26 months
December 31, 1957...	August 31, 1959	433.5	664.0	+53.2 in 20 months
July 31, 1962.......	August 31, 1965	585.5	896.0	+53.0 in 37 months
November 30, 1966..	December 31, 1967	789.0	896.0	+13.6 in 13 months
July 31, 1970.......	August 31, 1971	733.0	909.0	+24.0 in 13 months
October 31, 1974....	October 31, 1975	666.0	836.5	+25.6 in 12 months
Average Gain.....				40.5 in 20.2 months

been 40.5 percent for an average holding period of 20.2 months. Table 5–7 details these results. Because of this accuracy, the Market Barometer is an important tool in helping us define when to employ specific option strategies.[2]

[2] Note: The Market Barometer's readings plus several other special timing tools are available through the *Market Timing Report* published twice monthly by Cowen & Company, 209 South LaSalle Street, Chicago, Ill. 60604. In addition to this report the figures are published in Gerald Appel's, *Systems and Forecasts*, Signalert Corporation, Box 1212, Old Village Station, Great Neck, N.Y. 11023.

For those desiring to construct a Market Barometer, a simple approximation can be generated by selecting a sample of 100 major companies from the R. W. Mansfield weekly basis charts covering New York Stock Exchange issues. The first part of the sample comes from pages 1 and 2, followed by two or more stocks from the

However, to make money in the stock market, more precise measures are needed than the market barometer. Through experience with the market's crowd psychology, several measures have been developed to deal with the swings in sentiment which so aptly describe price behavior. These techniques essentially measure something that the random walkers call "drift," or an extended price movement in a given direction. If measured properly, these "drifts" tend to possess limits which correspond to either overly bullish crowd sentiment or the reverse. A graph of the measure for 5- to 30-week price swings (the average is 14 weeks) is presented in Figure 5–4. To indicate the lack of randomness, the record of buy and sell signals for this method are presented in Table 5–8. The odds of just simply getting the price direction correct after each signal if this were a random process would be 0.0000002!!

A similar technique has been developed for catching shorter-term price swings in the range of 5 to 20 trading days. A sample for the period December 1, 1973, through July 31, 1974, is

---

major industry groups such as airlines, aerospace, etc. Choose the stocks with the most shares outstanding. Then, each month take a nose count of the slopes of the 30-week moving averages. Use a clear plastic ruler to see whether the most recent two months of the moving average show a slope of greater than 10 percent if extended forward a year. This is an uptrend stock. Worse than 10-percent deterioration is a downtrend. The residual readings are the neutral stocks. Smoothing the monthly totals with a four-month moving average should yield results very close to the published version.

FIGURE 5-4

The Intermediate Cycle Measure versus the Dow Jones Industrial Average

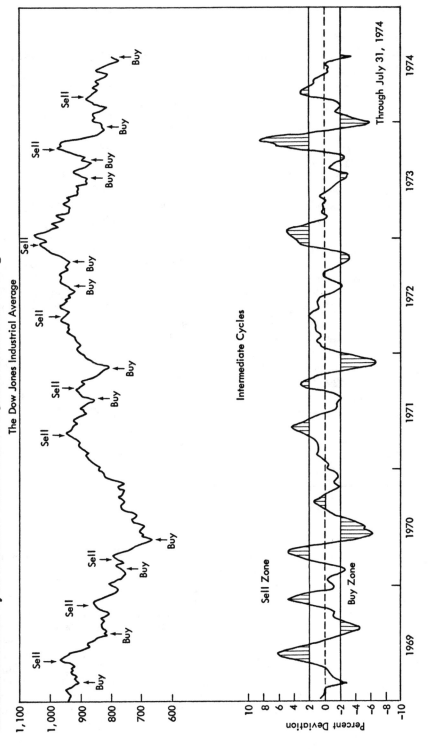

The Dow Jones Industrial Average

Intermediate Cycles

Through July 31, 1974

TABLE 5–8

Intermediate Buy and Sell Signals for January 1, 1969, through July, 1974

	Date Signal Given	Buy	Sell	Points Profit (loss)	Percent Profit (loss)
1.	March 7, 1969	916.37			
2.	May 9, 1969		963.00	46.63	5.1
3.	August 1, 1969	824.23		138.77	14.4
4.	November 7, 1969		856.88	32.65	4.0
5.	February 20, 1970	766.54		90.34	10.5
6.	March 27, 1970		788.14	21.60	2.8
7.	May 22, 1970	665.66		122.48	15.5
8.	April 23, 1971		946.67	281.01	42.2
9.	August 13, 1971	890.11		56.56	6.0
10.	September 17, 1971		897.96	7.85	0.9
11.	November 12, 1971	817.24		80.72	9.0
12.	April 28, 1972		942.28	125.04	15.3
13.	July 28, 1972	937.24		5.04	0.5
14.	October 13, 1972	931.90			
15a	December 15, 1972		1,009.07	71.83*	7.7
15b	December 15, 1972		1,009.07	77.17†	7.6
16.	June 29, 1973	874.18		134.89	13.4
17.	September 7, 1973	888.40			
18a	October 5, 1973		956.80	82.62*	9.4
18b	October 5, 1973		956.80	68.40†	7.7
19.	December 14, 1973	826.03		130.77	13.7
20.	March 29, 1974		852.32	26.29	3.2
21.	July 19, 1974	794.62		57.70	6.8

* From first buy.
† From second buy.

presented in Figure 5–5. In this case a sequence of 17 successful signals was given.[3]

---

[3] The timing cycles for the intermediate and trading swings are generated by a measurement called an inverse moving average. For the intermediate term a 30-week moving average of the Dow Jones Industrial Average is computed, using the mean weekly price for each data point. The moving average is centered by plotting the most recent value 15 weeks behind the latest DJIA value. The inverse moving average is derived by then subtracting the centered moving average value from the 15-week-

FIGURE 5–5

The Trading Cycles versus the Dow Jones Industrial Average

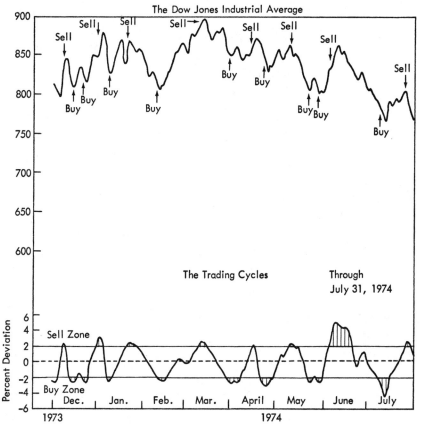

old DJIA point on the graph directly above or below and expressing this difference as a percent of the centered moving average. To bring the measurement up to date in order to characterize the most recent DJIA point, the centered moving average must be extrapolated forward by projecting a line through the most recent five centered moving average points, using this projection to obtain a current percent deviation. A similar technique is used for the trading cycle, except that a 30-day centered moving average is used along with the mean daily prices of the Dow Jones Industrial Average.

Those market students who wish to delve into such techniques in depth should obtain a copy of *The Profit*

But so much for price swings. How about the fundamental and psychological influences which were the driving forces for the swings? This is such a complex subject that volumes of books would be required to analyze only some of the driving forces and behavioral patterns involved. However, the key to understanding the process is one word, profits. And it is not just the actual profit numbers themselves, but how our market crowd perceives the likely future level of profits. Many factors can shape this perception, but for the most part it is very similar to the race track; the vast majority of people depend on the touts. It is painful to be an individual. It takes endless

---

Magic of Stock Transaction Timing by J. M. Hurst, Englewood Cliffs, N.J.: Prentice-Hall.

For those investors who have trouble performing the extrapolations necessary for the inverse moving average, several other techniques have been developed which require no extrapolation. The intermediate cycle measure is performed as follows:

1. Using average weekly prices for the Dow Jones Industrial Average, compute the relative percent change between the latest week's data and the average price three weeks prior to that.
2. Smooth this relative percent change by multiplying the most recent four weeks of changes by 0.1, 0.2, 0.3, and 0.4, with 0.4 applied to the most recent point. The sum of these four weighted readings is the value of the index for the latest week.
3. The index is used as an oscillator, a buy signal being generated by a downturn from above the zero line, a sell signal given by an upturn from below the zero line as shown below:

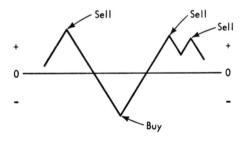

hours of exhausting research to carefully arrive at your own conclusions.

Human nature and the natural law of accomplishing something with the least effort possible determine that most people are followers. Who then are the opinion makers? They can be political leaders, the Chairman of the Federal Reserve, banking leaders, business leaders, the writers of investment advisory letters, the writers of Wall Street research, or well-known money managers. All these people, and more, communicate their ideas and feelings to the market crowd through the news media, especially the *Wall Street Journal, Barron's National Business and Financial Weekly,* and the *Wall Street Transcript.*

Their efforts regarding an appraisal of the future level of corporate profits have to deal with the societal system within which a business operates. If money is going to be tight, businesses will be denied credit, so that they might get into

---

The trading cycle uses a similar technique with average daily prices of the Dow Jones Industrial Average. In this case, the computations are as follows:

1. Compute the relative percent change between today's average price and the price four trading days prior to it.
2. Smooth the four most recent computations by multiplying them by 0.1, 0.2, 0.3, and 0.4, respectively, with the most recent percent change receiving the 0.4 weight. The sum of these four weighted readings gives the latest value of the trading index.
3. The trading index is used as an oscillator in the same manner as the intermediate measure, a sell signal being given by a downturn from plus territory, the buy signal given by an upturn from negative territory.

Readers should find these measures surprisingly well behaved. They are also applicable to individual stock prices.

trouble through the higher cost of credit, or they may even go bankrupt if they can't pay their bills. If the government begins restricting the freedom of businesses, either overall or in a given industry, the level of profits will usually be threatened. Therefore, widely accepted fears that this will occur will depress affected stock prices.

Possibly the best means of understanding this process is to first learn in what kind of an environment a business prospers and then the environment in which business suffers. This can be based on personal experience or by observing what happens to different businesses under various sets of conditions. Then, the trick is to read the appropriate financial media to determine how all the opinion makers perceive the current environment. If you perceive a change taking place that the opinion makers haven't begun to talk about, and the stock price behavior supports your viewpoint, you are probably early in a particular price movement. If the idea warrants front page treatment, especially in the general news media such as the *New York Times*, the crowd is also aware of the development and you are most likely late in a price progression. This is the process, and unfortunately it is not easy to teach. The interested student will have to study and experience for himself for many years until he understands the process enough to function profitably. Fortunately there are option strategies which circumvent the need for such in-depth study, but they offer a modest return on investment. The greater rewards require harder work.

The foregoing comments are not meant to communicate a feeling of hopelessness, because fortunately the major psychological inputs can be organized and measured to a degree. The following analysis is an attempt to put such order in an otherwise confusing world of market developments.

A financial editor once made the statement that even Albert Einstein could never design an equation to describe stock price behavior because there would be a near infinite number of variables and the interrelationships would be too complex and ever changing. He is probably correct, but what about designing a weekly equation based on the major factors being considered by the market opinion makers? Table 5–9 presents just such an analysis for the week of July 21, 1974. The important variables are ranked by order of importance from the most important, credit system instability, all the way down to the foreign exchange rate of the dollar. The ranking is determined by measuring both the frequency of occurrence of such items in the financial news media, and the impact on price changes in the marketplace as the news items are published in the *Dow Jones News Ticker*. The trend of the variables is listed for each variable, as well as the price effect. This is done to assist in determining whether the effect of the variable is likely to continue or whether a change in direction is taking place. The price effect is stressed because too often the effect is opposite to what most analysts might think. For example, at times the evidence of price inflation

TABLE 5–9

The Psychological Equation

Variable	Current Direction	Price Effect
1. Credit system* instability	Negative	Negative
2. Interest rates*	Near-term trend up, but possibly turning	Positive. if interest rates do, in fact, turn down
3. Dow Jones Industrial Average	Positive near-term	Positive
4. Brokerage house profitability	Negative	Negative
5. Rate of inflation	Rate moderating from recent excessive levels	Positive
6. Presidential crisis	Negative	Negative
7. International oil prices	Beginning to drop	Positive
8. Middle East peace	Positive	Positive if progress on Syrian Israeli disengagement
9. Corporate profits	Increasing at a decreasing rate	Positive for positive earnings changes, negative if earnings change is negative
10. GNP growth	Growth rate negative	Negative as indication that economy is slowing
11. Foreign exchange rate of dollar	Somewhat stronger	Positive if dollar rises, negative if dollar falls

* Credit system instability and interest rates continue to dominate the investing scene. A true market recovery continues to depend on these two key variables.

is a positive driving force when the opinion leaders are preaching buying stocks because they are a hedge against inflation. At another time the opinion leaders may be gripped with fear about government interference in business to control inflation and therefore the greater the inflation, the lower stock prices. This concept is especially important because too many analysts are tempted to analyze market behavior with fixed logic, such as "inflation is bullish," while the world around them is operating on a completely different basis.

This psychological equation, as it is called, can assist in price prediction by focusing attention on the most relevant factors in the marketplace. If interest rates and stability of the world banking system are paramount, the stock price detective should be best served by seeking clues as to important changes in these areas. The person who has the best insight in these matters should come out at the top of the competitive heap in terms of correct market judgments.

The true importance of the psychological equation is that it helps explain the major shifts in sentiment which so characterize market behavior. Contrary to the believers in a perfect market, the major driving forces move in cycle-like behavior, first offering the appearance that all is well with the world, causing a market rally, then reversing or becoming less positive to end the advance or even trigger a rout. The announcement of the Arab oil embargo in October 1973 didn't drop the Dow Jones Industrial Average 200 points in one day; it caused a 200-point decline until the beginning of December as the true impact of the decision began to manifest itself. Yet, there were experienced money managers who understand the market's abhorrence of a major negative development of unknown proportions and who sold a great deal of stock in October to successfully avoid the "perfect market's" six-week slump. The part of such behavior that throws the random walkers off guard is that fact that these shifts in sentiment occur at randomly spaced intervals and exhibit a wide degree of price change between shifts. The trick is to recognize the cycle-like turn as it is occurring. The psychological equation will assist in recognizing this as will the monitoring of opinion maker sentiment. In October 1973, a great deal of money had been spent on a widely accepted thesis that there would be a worldwide shortage in many basis raw materials for years to come. There was near unanimity that prices were headed much higher, the perfect description of a cyclical top. And six weeks later, at the height of the oil embargo, there was near universal despair about the future of the Western World, thus a cyclical low. It is almost as simple as that the market needs good news to drive prices up and with no news or bad news prices will fall. And, if the psychology has reached one of its poles, the market will even invent an excuse to change direction. This is what Gerald Loeb means by "the market makes the news." How does one capitalize on these swings in sentiment to make money? While this depends on the strategy as well as the magnitude of the price move expected, the tactic is essentially to use the market swings as a guide to establishing or unwinding positions. The criteria for stock selection depend so much on the option strategy employed that this will be covered in detail for each of the strategies discussed in the chapters which follow.

But, to demonstrate the effectiveness of using the market swings, a study of the price movement of five CBOE stocks, selected in alphabetical order from every seventh stock listed in the *Wall Street Journal* quotes, is analyzed in Table 5–10 versus the intermediate buy signals of Table 5–8. Even without any regard for the existence of a bull market or a bear market, 81 of the 100 price moves occurred in the predicted direction, and the average gains exceeded the average losses in all cases. This should offer some credence to the methodology presented in this chapter, namely, the cross-checking of crowd behavior with price swings to determine whether the market is at a cycle-like turning point.

Fortunately the individual is not completely alone in his analysis of price movements. The *Value Line Investment Survey* does an excellent job of presenting pertinent fundamental statistics for more than 1,800 leading companies, along with the most important company developments as reported by their staff or security analysts. *Investors Intelligence* offers a service which monitors the degree of bullishness or bearishness from a sample of leading advisory services, and Perry Wysong, in his *Insiders/ Specialist* report, tracks the behavior of the New York Stock Exchange specialists who reflect in their behavior the swings in market sentiment discussed in this chapter.[4] All of these services are advertised each week in *Barron's*.

---

[4] Perry Wysong, *Consensus of Insiders*, P.O. Box 10247, Fort Lauderdale, Fla. 33305.

TABLE 5–10

The Effect of Market Buy and Sell Signals on Five Randomly Selected CBOE Stocks

Date/Signal		AT&T Price	AT&T Percent Profit (loss)	Exxon Price	Exxon Percent Profit (loss)	Int'l Harvester Price	Int'l Harvester Percent Profit (loss)	Monsanto Price	Monsanto Percent Profit (loss)	Texas Instruments Price	Texas Instruments Percent Profit (loss)
March 7, 1969,	Buy	51¾		79⅛		33⅞		47⅝		102¾	
May 9, 1969,	Sell	57¼	+10.6	84	+ 6.2	32½	− 4.1	48⅞	+ 2/6	123⅝	+20.3
Aug. 1, 1969,	Buy	52¼	+ 8.7	72¼	+14.0	29⅛	+10.4	45¼	+ 7.4	118¼	+ 4.3
Nov. 7, 1969,	Sell	53½	+ 2.4	65⅛	− 9.9	28	− 3.9	41	− 9.4	125¾	+ 6.3
Feb. 20, 1970,	Buy	50¼	+ 6.1	54⅞	+15.7	27½	+ 1.8	32⅛	+21.6	129¾	− 2.8
March 27, 1970,	Sell	52¾	+ 5.0	57¾	+ 5.2	28½	+ 3.6	34¾	+ 8.2	119	− 7.9
May 22, 1970,	Buy	43½	+17.5	51¼	+11.3	23¼	+22.6	29½	+15.1	83⅝	+29.7
April 23, 1971,	Sell	48⅝	+11.8	81	+58.0	28⅛	+21.0	44¾	+51.7	116	+38.7
Aug. 13, 1971,	Buy	44½	+ 8.5	70½	+13.0	28⅜	− 0.9	46	− 2.8	113	+ 2.6
Sept. 17, 1971,	Sell	42⅝	− 4.2	71⅜	+ 1.2	28⅛	− 0.9	50¼	+ 9.2	114	+ 0.9
Nov. 12, 1971,	Buy	42¼	+ 0.9	67⅞	+ 4.9	25	+11.1	44⅛	+12.2	104	+ 8.8
April 28, 1972,	Sell	42⅞	+ 1.5	69⅝	+ 2.6	30⅞	+23.5	54⅜	+23.2	149⅞	+44.1
July 28, 1972,	Buy	41¾	+ 2.6	75⅞	− 9.0	33	− 6.9	49¾	+ 8.5	171⅝	−14.5
Oct. 13, 1972,	Buy	47⅝		81¾		36		49⅛		164⅜	
Dec. 15, 1972,	Sell	51¾	+24.0	86⅛	+13.5	39¼	+18.9	50¾	+ 2.0	170¼	− 0.8
Dec. 15, 1972,	Sell	51¾	+ 8.7	86⅛	+ 5.4	39¼	+ 8.3	50¾	+ 3.3	170¼	+ 3.6
June 29, 1973,	Buy	50⅞	+ 1.7	98¼	−14.1	27¼	+30.6	51¼	− 1.0	83⅝*	+ 1.8
Sept. 7, 1973,	Buy	48⅞		87¼		32¾		60⅛		108⅝	
Oct. 5, 1973,	Sell	51⅜	+ 1.0	93⅝	− 4.7	35⅛	+28.9	75¼	+46.8	131¼	+57.0
Oct. 5, 1973,	Sell	51⅜	+ 8.6	93⅝	+ 7.3	35⅛	+ 7.3	75¼	+25.2	131¼	+20.8
Dec. 14, 1973,	Buy	48½	+ 5.6	90¾	+ 3.2	23½	+33.1	45½	+39.5	94⅝	+27.9
March 29, 1974,	Sell	49⅛	+ 1.3	80¾	−11.6	27⅝	+17.6	57⅛	+25.5	95⅛	+ 0.53
July 19, 1974,	Buy	43¾	+10.9	75¾	+ 5.6	23⅜	+15.4	63⅛	−10.5	87⅛	+ 8.4
No. of Profitable Transactions		19		15		15		16		16	
Average Profit		7.2%		11.1%		16.9%		18.9%		17.2%	
No. Of Loss Transactions		1		5		5		4		4	
Average Loss		4.2%		9.9%		3.3%		5.9%		6.5%	

* Split 2 for 1.

If the eager student wants to become well versed in the art of understanding the stock market as detailed in this chapter he should read *The Wall Street Journal* daily and subscribe to *Business Week, Barron's Fortune* magazine, and possibly *Forbes*. In this manner he will at least become conversant with the jargon of Wall Street and most of the major ideas that are driving prices back and forth in the marketplace.

The High Risk/High Reward Strategies

6

Attempting success with these techniques is the climbing of Mount Everest among the various option strategies. While they are most tempting because of the large profit potential when an investor is correct, they are also the most demanding in terms of timing skills, the ability to make sound and rapid judgments and, most difficult of all, the discipline to properly manage your capital. As we mentioned in the chapter on setting strategies, the objective is not simply to make a profit but to operate defensively enough so that you can survive a string of mistakes and still have capital enough to make another trade.

While the market barometer can be a helpful guide in terms of deciding whether to use a bull market or a bear market strategy, some more specific timing tools will be required if one is to be successful. With this in mind the following techniques are presented as an aid. The techniques differ from most methods promoted by books on technical analysis which suggest taking action the moment an uptrend or downtrend line such as that drawn between points 1 and 2 in Figure 6–1 is penetrated. The alternate method

FIGURE 6–1

A. Detecting a Change in an Uptrend and Selling a Long Position

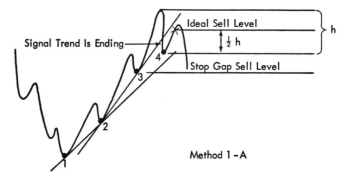

B. Detecting a Change in a Downtrend and Covering Short

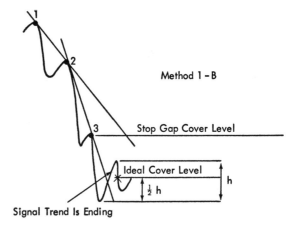

suggested here is to draw trendlines connecting successive troughs for uptrend stocks and using the penetration of the most current of these trendlines only as a signal that a change is taking place. Roughly 70 percent of the time the price will not move past the point marked 3, but will reverse and resume its original direction. The distance from highest point in the uptrend and that reversal point 4 gives the measurement of where to sell, one-half of the distance from the highest price to point 4. The reverse is true for the downtrend. In this manner the investor allows the market to come to his price level. This is an important advantage because the commonplace approach of chasing a market that is running away from you is avoided. And to protect yourself in case the price doesn't reverse, the previous turning point 3 is used as a stopgap level to either sell or cover short. In this manner the investor is protected against all eventualities.

The technique for either buying or selling short is a slight variation of the foregoing method. (See Figure 6–2) In the case of buying into a new uptrend, the same procedure is used of drawing downtrend lines along successive pairs of price peaks with the first penetration of a downtrend line signaling that a change in direction may be taking place. Confirmation of the change is a trough (5) which is higher than the previous trough (4), the buy point being the first point where the formation of trough (5) is detected. In case this is a false signal, the position should be resold if the price drops more than one average trading day's range below the turning point (5).

To sell short, the reverse of the foregoing method is used. In this case the short point is the first point that a peak (5) lower than the highest peak in the trend (4) can be clearly recognized. A short covering point should be established at

FIGURE 6–2

A. Buying into a New Uptrend

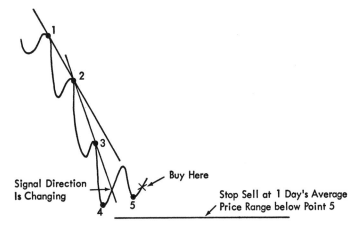

B. Selling Short into a New Downtrend

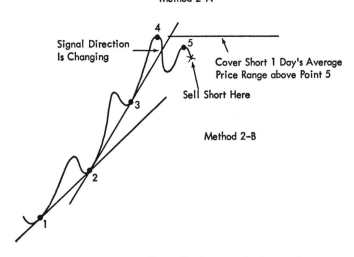

one average trading day's range above the turning point (5).

To avoid false signals several rules should be followed. One is that penetration of a trendline should be evidenced by an entire day's trading range on the other side of the trendline from where prices have been. Another is that an average daily trading range should be judged by inspection of a daily basis vertical line chart or better by computation of an average of the previous ten days' trading ranges. Once action has been taken either buying or selling short, the position should be maintained until a contrary signal for taking action occurs. In this manner if you are blessed with a large move in your favor, you should enjoy those large profits. The usual tendency of making an emotional judgment proves invariably to be wrong. The demanding prerequisite is to have the patience to allow these signals to occur, rather than anticipating what will occur and jumping the gun.

Several actual examples of the foregoing methods are presented in Figures 6–3 and 6–4 to demonstrate that the timing techniques do work for CBOE stocks. The important point to be remembered is that a predetermined measurement should be established to cover all eventualities. It is tempting to think that you will never be wrong, especially if you have enjoyed a string of successes, but you should be prepared at all times for a reversal. If you follow these general guidelines, you will be applying the well-worn Wall Street maxim of letting your profits run and cutting your losses short. What is usually left out is the method to accomplish those ends. With these procedures the option investor should be on sound footing.

Before going on to the rules for the specific strategies, a chart of the Dow Jones Industrial Average will be analyzed for the period of May

FIGURE 6-3

A. Example of Selling at the End of an Uptrend

B. Example of Covering Short at the End of a Downtrend

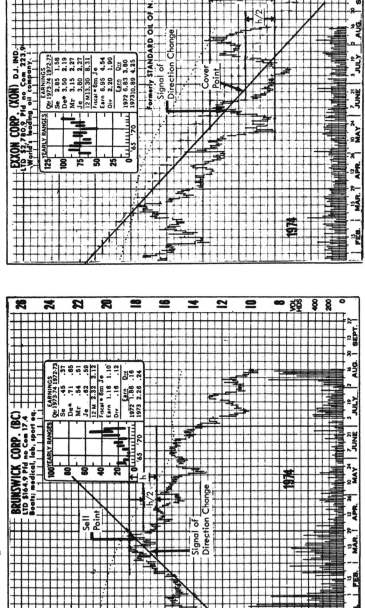

FIGURE 6–4

A. Example of Buying at the Beginning of a New Uptrend

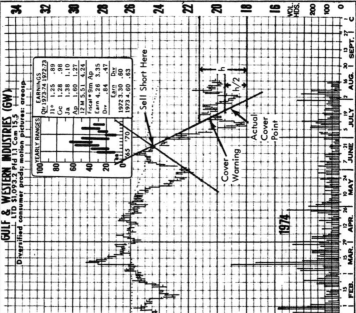

B. Example of Selling Short at the Beginning of a New Downtrend

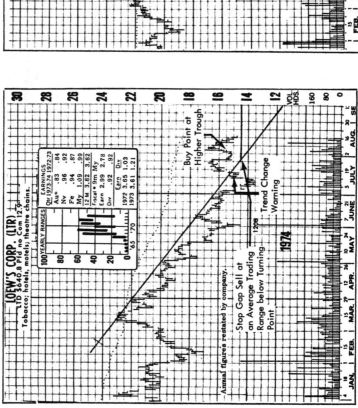

FIGURE 6–5

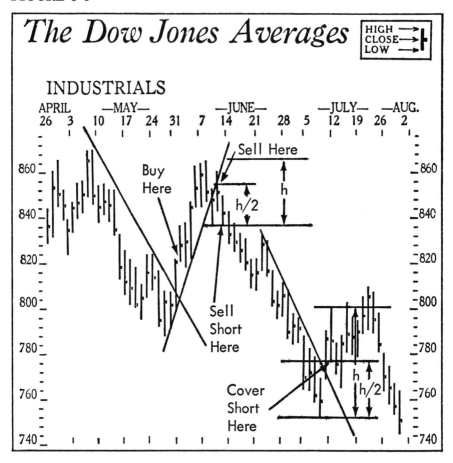

through July, 1974, just to demonstrate the general application of the price trend measuring techniques presented in this chapter. The graph used for Figure 6–5 was taken from the inside back page of the *Wall Street Journal.*

The first buy signal was given by the index's first penetrating a downtrend line, thus signaling the change in direction, and then rallying above the previous peak. This is the exception occurring, as the index failed to drop back to the $\frac{1}{2} h$ level. The sell signal which occurred next worked according to the odds and yielded a profit from the buy point. A sell short signal was given immediately thereafter. The cover short signal also worked according to the usual pattern, yielding a profit which capitalized on nearly 80 percent of the drop. Some traders may prefer to do this type of market average analysis as a cross check against their individual stock work, preferring to execute trades in sympathy with general market moves. This, in fact, is the recommended procedure.

The first strategies to be treated will be the high risk/high reward methods to be applied in a bull market. These are buying calls and selling puts naked. Referring back to the chapter on price behavior, a bull market is one in which stocks with strong major uptrends dominate the market. For this reason, the stock selected should exhibit uptrend behavior as defined by successively rising peaks and troughs with ten or more weeks between each peak. A weekly basis stock chart service such as R. W. Mansfield's, 26 Journal Square, Jersey City, New Jersey, is an ideal tool for such a screen. For buying calls the suggested procedure is as follows:

1. Buy calls only in a bull market as determined by the measurements of the market barometer.
2. Select those stocks with major uptrend behavior and with healthy fundamentals. Avoid a controversial situation.

3. The point to make a commitment is at the end of an intermediate length decline (5 to 20 weeks) as signalled by Perry Wysong's *Specialist Analysis* or a methodology similar to that presented in Chapter 5, which indicates that while crowd sentiment is extremely bearish after a decline, individual stock prices are beginning to improve.

4. Select your candidates from those exhibiting 20 percent or greater volatility as measured in Chapter 3.

5. Select four or five situations to diversify your position and protect against disappointment in a single commitment. The options should have a minimum of two to three months of life remaining and should have strike prices within 5 percent of the current price of the underlying stock.

6. Use buy signals such as those presented in this chapter for the underlying stock to time your purchase.

   a. when the signal is given, place buy orders for the options at the market price for the option plus a 1/16 point discretion on options trading at 1 or less, 1/8 point discretion for those above 1 up to 5, and a 1/4 point discretion above 5. Have your broker put the orders on the board broker's book.

7. Ideally, the option premium should be no more than 25 percent above fair value as determined from the pricing graphs in Chapter 3. The preference is for options trading below fair value.

8. Commit no more than 40 percent of your trading capital to your entire position. This money should be thought of as maximum risk capital, which could be entirely lost without changing your life-style one iota.

9. Each call commitment should be monitored daily by updating either a published set of stock charts, or your own, for each underlying stock, so that the position can be closed out as each stock reaches first its warning point, then the actual sell point.

By following these rules, the option trader should have the odds in his favor of making profits with a good degree of consistency, while avoiding most of the pitfalls which rob traders not only of their profits but their hard-earned capital as well.

The other high reward/high risk strategy for a bull market is the naked writing of puts. The objective of writing a put naked is to collect the put premium without ever having to honor the put contract. This contractual obligation requires the put seller (writer) to purchase 100 shares of the put's underlying stock at the strike price at any time during the life of the put. Quite naturally, as long as the underlying stock price remains at or above the strike price, there is no advantage for the put buyer to exercise his put. Logically, then, the put writer should want to write a put in the underlying stock of a well thought of, fundamentally healthy company, with a greater than fair value premium, at a time when the overall market and the underlying stock are beginning to rally. Since the put writer's obligation can be no more than the face value of the stock of the puts he writes, the writer should have a reserve, in case his timing judgment is wrong, of at least the collective face value of his put portfolio at their strike prices, less the put premiums he has received. A writer might argue that he can use margin in case he gets in trouble so that he doesn't need to completely cover all his put obligations, but this is highly dangerous. It is bad enough to lose your own capital, let alone some that you have borrowed. Once headed in this direction a string of mistakes is likely to occur and the losses on borrowed money could wipe out your capital. This comes back to the defense we stressed so heavily in Chapter 4. The overall goal should be to stay in the game, and not be taken out because of a few mistakes. Organizing this logic into a set of rules, we have:

1. Write puts only in a bull market as determined by the measurements of the market barometer.
2. Select as candidates puts whose underlying stocks are exhibiting major uptrend behavior, where the fundamental outlook is positive. Avoid a controversial situation.
3. The point at which to make the commitment is at the end of an intermediate-length decline (5 to 20 weeks) as signaled by Perry Wysong's *Specialist Analysis* or a methodology similar to the one suggested in Chapter 5.

4. The time to maturity should be no more than two to three months.
5. The options written should have premiums at least 50 percent greater than fair value.
6. The put-writing portfolio should be diversified to four or five different underlying stocks. The puts written should be trading with the underlying stock price at or above the strike price of the puts.
7. The writing commitment should be undertaken at the same time that a buy signal, such as described in this chapter, is given for the underlying stock. Place the orders at the market with $\frac{1}{16}$-point discretion for premiums of 1 or less, $\frac{1}{8}$-point discretion for premiums above 1 up to 5, and $\frac{1}{4}$-point discretion above 5. Have your broker place the orders on the board broker's book.
8. A fully invested position is one in which the capital plus premiums collected equals the total commitment to purchase the stock obligated to for the puts that were written.
9. Monitor the daily price action of the underlying stocks just as you would in the buy call strategy, closing out the position if a sell signal is given for the underlying stock.

An additional measuring tool will be offered at this point as a means of aiding in the selection of the specific options for the various trading strategies. This tool is the graph comparing the relative degree of price change in an option (whether a call or a put), depending on the current relationship of the strike price and the price

of the underlying stock. Presented in Figure
6–6, the diagram offers a means of determining
the point movement in a particular option relative to its underlying stock by defining first the
time to maturity of the option and the percent
difference between the option's strike price and
the price of the underlying stock. For example,
a three-month option trading at 20 percent below its strike price (read along the vertical
scale) would only move 20 percent of the point
movement in the underlying stock (read along
the horizontal scale). If the same option were
trading at the strike price, the point movement
would be 50 percent of that in the underlying
stock. The importance of this diagram is to indicate that for trading moves, a call trading at 20
percent or more below the strike price would
have to enjoy a 10-point move in the underlying
stock to move 2 points.

Even if the price of the option (the premium)
is extremely low, the odds of enjoying a good
profit with an appreciable change in the underlying stock price may also be low. A safer bet
would be an option trading above the strike
price, where the price sensitivity of the option
would be better than half of the point change in
the underlying stock.

The next high risk/high reward strategies to
be considered are those to be employed in a bear
market as determined by the market barometer.
Buying puts is the first such strategy to be considered and should be thought of as an alternative to selling short, the advantage of the put being the fact that if he is wrong, the put buyer

FIGURE 6–6

Comparison of Option Price Change with Underlying Stock Price and Time to Maturity

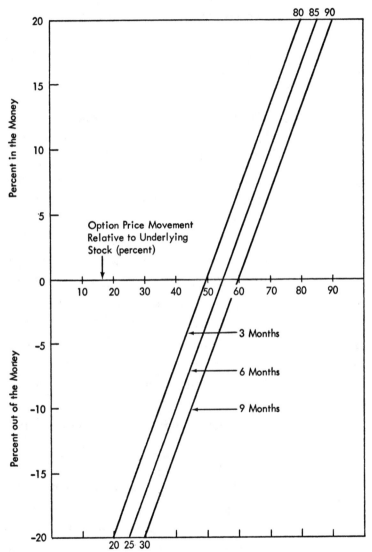

merely loses the premium he paid for the option. The short seller incurs a risk that is limited only by how high a stock can rally.

The rules for buying puts are as follows:

1. Buy puts only in a bear market as determined by the measurement of the market barometer.
2. Select those stocks with major downtrend behavior and with deteriorating fundamentals. A controversial situation is a good choice, as many investors having doubts about the company's future will prefer to pull to the sidelines; i.e., they will sell.
3. The point at which to make a commitment is at the end of an intermediate-length rally (5 to 20 weeks), as signaled by Perry Wysong's *Specialist Analysis* or a methodology similar to that presented in Chapter 5, which indicates that while crowd sentiment is extremely positive after on advance, individual stock prices are beginning to deteriorate.
4. Select your candidates from those exhibiting 20-percent or greater volatility as measured in Chapter 3.
5. Select four or five situations to diversify your position and protect against disappointment in a single commitment. The options should have a minimum of two to three months of life remaining and should have strike prices within 5 percent of the current price of the underlying stock.
6. Use sell signals such as presented in this

chapter for the underlying stock to time your purchase.

a. when the signal is given, place buy orders for the options at the market price for the option plus a $\frac{1}{16}$-point discretion on options trading at 1 or less, $\frac{1}{8}$-point discretion for those above 1 up to 5, and a $\frac{1}{4}$-point discretion above 5. Have your broker put the orders on the board broker's book.

7. Ideally, the option premium should be no more than 25 percent above fair value as determined from the pricing graphs in Chapter 3, using 80 percent of the call premium as an estimate of the fair-value put premium. The preference is for options trading below fair value.

8. Commit no more than 40 percent of your trading capital to your entire position. This money should be thought of as maximum risk capital, which could be entirely lost without changing your life-style one iota.

9. Each put commitment should be monitored daily, by updating either a published set of stock charts, or your own, for each underlying stock so that the position can be closed out as each stock reaches first its warning point and then the actual short covering point.

The other high reward/high risk strategy for a bear market is the naked writing of calls. The objective is for the calls to expire unexercised so that the investor does not have to honor the call obligation if they are exercised. The defense in this case is the limiting of the position to the amount of money, including the call premiums received, needed to honor the calls if every one was exercised. If done correctly, this eventuality should rarely arise. However, the intelligent investor should be prepared for the worst. The rules for writing calls naked are as follows:

1. Write calls only in a bear market as determined by the measurements of the market barometer.
2. Select as candidates calls whose underlying stocks are exhibiting major downtrend behavior, in which the fundamental outlook is negative. A controversial situation is usually a good choice.
3. The point at which to make the commitment is at the end of an intermediate-length rally (5 to 20 weeks) as signaled by Perry Wysong's *Specialist Analysis* or a methodology similar to the one suggested in Chapter 5.
4. The time to maturity should be no more than two to three months.
5. The options written should have premiums at least 50 percent greater than fair value as determined by the premium-pricing curves of Chapter 3.
6. The call-writing portfolio should be diversified to four or five different underlying stocks. The calls written should be trading with the underlying stock price at or below the strike price of the calls.

7. The writing commitment should be undertaken at the same time that a sell signal
   such as described in this chapter is given
   for the underlying stock. Place the order at
   the market with ¹⁄₁₆-point discretion for
   premiums of 1 or less, ⅛-point discretion
   for premiums above 1 up to 5, and ¼-point
   discretion above 5. Have your broker place
   the orders on the board broker's book.
8. A fully invested position is one in which the
   capital plus premiums collected equals the
   total commitment to purchase and deliver
   the stock obligated to for which the calls
   were written.
9. Monitor the daily price action of the underlying stocks just as you would in the buy-
   put strategy, closing out the position if a
   short cover signal is given for the underlying stock.

In choosing one of these strategies, the investor should experiment with one or the other until
he finds which one he is most comfortable with
for a given market environment. He should then
stick to that strategy, perfecting his skill until
his capital has been built up to a substantial
enough amount and he desires a safer, more defensive, strategy, or until the price environment
changes from bullish to bearish. This procedure
is recommended because switching back and
forth from one strategy to another will never allow the investor to become truly proficient at
making money with a high degree of consistency. The investor may note that following the

foregoing rules may require him to sit in cash during a bull market or a bear market, waiting for the ideal climate to establish a position. This is one of the great keys to success. It is the emotionally spurred search for constant action that causes the vast majority of losses. This is where the demands of patience and discipline are most crucial.

The Moderate Risk/
Moderate Reward
Strategies

7

While requiring good timing and selection skills, the strategies covered in this chapter are far less high strung than those of Chapter 6. The two bull market strategies are:

1. Buying stock coupled with the purchase of a put for protection in case the stock declines.
2. Writing calls and purchasing an equivalent amount of stock, the goal being to collect the call premiums in order to augment the capital appreciation in the stock.

The two bear market strategies are:

1. Shorting stock while purchasing a call for protection in case the stock rallies.
2. Writing puts while shorting an equivalent amount of stock as a protected means of making money on the decline in a stock's price. The goal is to augment capital gains from the stock's decline by collecting put premiums.

Shorting stock, buying a call for protection and purchasing stock, buying a put for protection, emphasize the stock side of the transaction and are mainly a more defensive means of trading stocks than simply dealing in stocks alone. The mechanics of the procedure are probably best demonstrated with a few numerical examples.

Buying a Stock and Protecting the Stock by Purchasing a Put.
Case 1

A. The stock advances substantially and the position is closed out.

February 1

	Debit	Credit
Purchase 100 shares XYZ Corp. @$50 a share................	$5,000	
Purchase a 6-month put in XYZ Corp. with a strike price of $50 for $500.................	500	

April 1

The stock has risen to $60 a share and the investor decides to close out the position with a substantial profit.

	Debit	Credit
Resell 100 shares XYZ Corp. @ $60 a share................		$6,000

The investor decides to hold the put which is trading at $\frac{1}{16}$, as it may gain in value if the stock declines in price during the four months remaining in its life, or if the stock declines to a buy area near the put's strike price, the holder may wish to repeat the transaction. The result for the transaction is:

	Debit	Credit
Proceeds	$6,000	
Less cost of stock		$5,000
Less cost of put		500
Gross profit	$ 500	

$$\frac{\text{Gross profit}}{\text{Total capital outlay}} = \frac{\$\ 500}{\$5,500} \times 100$$
$$= 9.1\% \text{ return on capital in two months}$$

B. The stock is virtually unchanged during the six-month life of the put.

February 1

	Debit	Credit
Purchase 100 shares XYZ Corp. @ $50 a share	$5,000	
Purchase a 6-month put in XYZ Corp. with a strike price of $50 for $500		500

July 31

The stock price is unchanged and the option is worthless, since there is no advantage to exercising a put option at $50 a share if all that it allows a purchaser to do is buy stock selling at $50 and deliver it to the put writer for $50. The result for the transaction would be a cost of $500 for the put option which expired worthless. There would be no advantage in reselling the stock at the same price, so that the $500 put premium can be thought of as a cost of insuring the stock position for six months or

$$\frac{\text{Put cost}}{\text{Capital outlay}} = \frac{\$\ 500}{\$5,500} \times 100 = 9.1\%$$
$$\text{reduction in capital during six months}$$

C. The stock drops substantially and the holder of the 100 shares of XYZ decides to close out the position before it deteriorates further.

February 1

	Debit	Credit
Purchase 100 shares XYZ Corp. @ $50 a share................	$5,000	
Purchase a 6-month put in XYZ Corp. with a strike price of $50 for $500..................	500	

The stock drops in price to $40 a share in two months and the put appreciates in value to $1,100. The investor decides that the situation will probably deteriorate further and therefore decides to close out his position.

April 1

	Debit	Credit
Resell 100 Shares of XYZ Corp. @ $40 a share................		$4,000
Resell 1 put XYZ Corp. @ $1,100..................		1,100

The results of the total transactions are:

Proceeds from sale of stock........	$4,000	
Proceeds from sale of put.........	1,100	
Total proceeds..............	$5,100	
Less cost of 100 shares XYZ @ 50........................	$5,000	
Less cost of 1 put XYZ Corp......	500	
	$5,500	
Loss for transaction..............($	400)	

$$\text{Loss on position} = \frac{\text{Loss}}{\text{Capital outlay}}$$

$$= \frac{-\$400}{\$5,500} \times 100 = -7.3\% \text{ in 2 months}$$

D. The stock falls gradually during the life

of the option until the expiration date, when the investor decides to exercise his put and deliver his stock to the option writer.

February 1

	Debit	Credit
Purchase 100 shares XYZ Corp. @ $50 a share..........	$5,000	
Purchase a 6-month put in XYZ Corp. with a strike price of $50 for $500..........	500	

The stock gradually drops to $40 a share during the six month life of the put, and the investor decides to exercise.

July 31

	Debit	Credit
Deliver 100 shares of XYZ to the put writer for a price of $50 a share (the strike price)......................		$5,000

The results of the transaction are:

Proceeds from sale of stock......		$5,000
Less cost of 100 shares XYZ @ 50......................	5,000	
Less cost of 1 put XYZ Corp.....	500	$5,500
Loss for transaction............		($ 500)

$$\text{Loss on position} = \frac{\text{Loss}}{\text{Capital outlay}}$$

$$= \frac{-\$500}{\$5,500} \times 100 = -9.1\% \text{ in 6 months}$$

The important concept to be understood for this strategy is that the largest loss an investor can sustain if the position aborts is the cost of the put premium plus any difference between the strike price of the put and the price of the stock when the position was established. Why this is so depends on the feature of the put option, which enables the holder of 100 shares of stock to deliver his stock to the put writer and receive the strike price of the put for his shares. The stock price could drop from 50 in our numerical example to a price of 5 during the life of the put, and the stock could still be delivered at $50 a share. If the stock had been purchased at $50, the only cost to the stock purchaser is the cost of the put and any commissions and fees involved in the trades. For someone who is probability conscious there is no better way to hedge a speculative purchase. And if the investor or his broker is alert, he may find very low cost options trading in the aftermarket which offer a far lower cost than the numerical example just given.

A set of rules which might be helpful for this strategy are as follows:

1. Since making a profit on a rise in a stock's price is the major emphasis of this strategy, it should only be applied in a bull market as defined by the market barometer.

2. The ideal time to establish such a position is at the termination of an intermediate decline as defined in the chapter on price behavior.

   a. For more precision, the timing techniques described in the last chapter should be helpful, both to establish the position and to at least close out the stock side of the transaction.

3. Since the major cost of the strategy is the cost of the put being used for protection, the investor should seek put premiums trading at or below fair value as measured by the pricing curves in Chapter 3.

   a. It should be possible to find situations in which a stock is trading at $52 a share, and a three-month put is available with a $50 strike price trading at $200. The cost is the in-money value of the put at the time and is a good example of the inexpensive put protection that can be obtained.

The bear market strategy of selling stock short[1] and buying calls for protection is an extremely sensible way to trade stocks as opposed to shorting stocks alone. Again, several numerical examples might be the best means of demonstrating the technique.

A. The stock advances substantially and the position is closed out.

Shorting Stock and Protecting the Position by Purchasing a Call. Case 2

---

[1] Selling short is a technique for making a profit on a stock's price decline. This is managed by borrowing someone else's stock and selling that stock immediately for what is hoped to be a high price. Later, if the price has declined, the short seller enters the market, purchases the stock at a low price and delivers it back to the lender with all dividends received. In this manner, the borrower of the stock has enjoyed the fruits of a change in price, while the lender of the stock, who facilitated the entire transaction, enjoys the dividends as well as an interest fee for the stock he lent.

February 1

	Debit	Credit
Sell short 100 shares XYZ Corp. @ $50 a share..........		$5,000
Purchase a 6 month call in XYZ Corp. with a strike price of $50 for $500..........	$ 500	

April 1

The stock has risen to $60 a share and the investor decides he had better close out the position and absorb a loss.

	Debit	Credit
Purchase 100 shares XYZ Corp. @ $60 a share covering short...............	$6,000	
Resell 1 call XYZ Corp. @ $1,100...................		$1,100

The overall result for the transaction is:

Proceeds from stock sale.........	$5,000
Proceeds from sale of call........	1,100
Total proceeds.............	$6,100
Less cost of stock when repurchased..................	$6,000
Less cost of call...............	500
Total cost.................	$6,500
Loss......................	($ 400)

The return on capital for the transaction is:

$$\frac{\text{Gross loss}}{\text{Capital outlay}} = \frac{-\$400}{\$5,500} \times 100$$
$$= 7.3\% \text{ loss of capital in 2 months}$$

B.   The stock advances during the life of the call and the investor decides to exercise his call option at the expiration date.

February 1

	Debit	Credit
Sell short 100 shares XYZ Corp. @ $50 a share..........		$5,000
Purchase a 6 months call in XYZ Corp. with a strike price of $50 for $500..........	$500	

July 31

The stock has gradually risen to $60 a share during the six-month life of the call and the investor decides to exercise the call by taking delivery of the 100 shares of XYZ Corp. at $50 and re-delivering to the person he borrowed the stock from.

	Debit	Credit
Exercise 1 call XYZ Corp. and take delivery of 100 shares of XYZ Corp. @ $50 a share...............	$5,000	

The overall result from the transaction is:

Proceeds from short sale.........		$5,000
Less cost of 1 call XYZ Corp.....	500	
Less cost of stock purchased on exercise..................	5,000	5,500
Loss on transaction.........		($ 500)

The return on capital for the transaction is:

$$\frac{\text{Gross loss}}{\text{Capital outlay}} = \frac{-\$500}{\$5,500} \times 100$$

$$= 9.1\% \text{ loss on capital in 6 months}$$

C.   The stock is virtually unchanged during the six-month life of the call.

February 1

	Debit	Credit
Sell short 100 shares XYZ Corp. @ $50 a share...........		$5,000
Purchase 1 call in XYZ Corp. with a strike price of $50 for $500.....................	$500	

July 31

The stock price is unchanged and the option is worthless, as there is no advantage in exercising at the same price as the strike price. The result is similar to the short stock-buy call strategy in that the call premium is the cost incurred for having a protected stock position for six months. The capital cost would be as follows:

$$\frac{\text{Call cost}}{\text{Capital outlay}} = \frac{\$500}{\$5,500} \times 100 = 9.1\%$$
reduction in capital during 6 months

D. The stock drops substantially and the holder of the 100 shares of XYZ decides to take his profit.

February 1

	Debit	Credit
Sell short 100 shares XYZ Corp. @ $50 a share...........		$5,000
Purchase 1 call in XYZ Corp. with a strike price of $50 for $500.....................	$500	

The stock drops in price to $40 a share in two months and the investor decides to take his profit. The call at this time is trading for $\frac{1}{16}$ ($6.25), but still has four months until expiration. Therefore, rather than selling the call, the investor de-

cides to hold it in the event that the stock rallies
and becomes an attractive short, the call once
again providing him protection for his short position.

April 1

	Debit	Credit
Purchase 100 shares XYZ Corp. @ $40 a share, covering short................	$4,000	

The overall result for the position is:

Proceeds........................		$5,000
Less cost of buying stock.........	$4,000	
Less cost of call.................	500	
Gross profit................		$ 500

$$\text{Return on profit} = \frac{\text{Gross profit}}{\text{Capital outlay}} = \frac{\$500}{\$5,500}$$
$$\times 100 = 9.1\% \text{ gain in capital in 2 months}$$

The important concept to be remembered for
this strategy is that the cost of the call, along
with any commissions involved, is the full extent
of the loss that the investor can incur. For any
investors who have ever attempted shorting this
should be a comforting realization. Since the potential loss for the short stock is limited only by
the extent that the stock can rise in price, selling
short can be a harrowing experience, especially
so with the bear market rallies as sharp and
dramatic as they are. If one considers the general fear of rallies which short traders have, it is
easy to understand why there is such a mad
scramble to cover short positions at the slightest
hint of a rally. If one uses the technique of buy-

ing a call when establishing a short position, it is possible to be cool-headed as one waits for the position to work. If the recommended procedure of shorting into the last stages of a bear market rally is followed, once it becomes clear that the market and your stock have resumed their decline, the call can even be resold at a small loss, while the short stock is allowed to enjoy the balance of its decline.

A suggested set of rules for this strategy follows:

1. Since the major objective of this strategy is to make profits by declines in stock prices, it should be applied only in a bear market as defined by the market barometer.
2. The ideal time to establish such a position is at the termination of an intermediate advance as defined in the chapter on price behavior.
   a. for more precision, the timing techniques described in the last chapter should be helpful, both in establishing the short position and especially in closing out the position on weakness rather than getting caught up in a short squeeze, as all too frequently happens.
3. The investor should seek to purchase calls which are trading at or below fair value as measured by the pricing curves presented in Chapter 3. The investor should also be on the lookout for special pricing situations, such as mentioned for buying puts, in which

the investor may be able to pay no more than the in-money value of the option.

Fully hedged call writing is probably the most widely known and most popular option strategy. It has been used for centuries by a small number of sophisticated investors who establish themselves as the bankers for the buyers of call options. Whether by writing calls against low-priced stock owned in an estate or by purchasing stock in order to write calls, these investors have reputedly been able to earn 15 to 25 percent pretax on their capital when averaged out over five or more years. The strategy's emphasis is to earn the premiums on the calls the writer guarantees. The stock which is purchased is thought of as a capital investment in the option writing business, just as a manufacturer would think of his steel plant as a means for producing steel for sale. Writing fully hedged means that one call for 100 shares is written for each 100 shares of stock owned by the writer. And while it might be tempting to be able to employ this strategy under all market conditions, the fact is that a bear market will cause serious erosion in the project's capital, in the form of the stock that is owned, which is difficult, if not impossible, to match through the call premiums that are collected due to falling prices. The best environment in which to operate this strategy is the bull market dominated by rising stock prices.

There are four possible conclusions for a

fully hedged call writing position, and rather than omitting commission costs as in past examples, the following cases will not only deal in actual transactions on the CBOE, but indicate all commissions and dividends involved in the possible outcomes.

A. Stock Is Up—
Call Exercised

Date	Action	Debit	Credit
June 1	Buy 1,000 BS* @ 29¼ plus commissions....	$29,613	
June 1	Sell 10 calls BS @ 30 exp. 1/31/74 for $400		
	each.................................		$ 4,000
	Less commissions.........................		(118)
Aug. 2	Receive dividend .40.....................		$ 400
Oct. 31	Receive dividend .40.....................		$ 400
Jan. 31	BS is over 30 and the calls are exercised:		
	Sell 1,000 BS @ 30 a/c call..............		$30,000
	Less commissions.........................		(370)

* BS is the symbol for Bethlehem Steel.

Return on Investment

Proceeds...............................	$29,630	($30,000 − $370)
Plus premium...........................	3,882	(4,000 − 118)
	$33,512	
Less cost.............	29,613	
Capital gain............................	$ 3,899	
Plus dividend income....................	800	
	$ 4,699	

$$\text{ROI} = \frac{\text{Total pretax profit}}{\text{Investment}}$$

$$= \frac{\$4,699}{\$29,613 - \$3,882} = 18.2\% \text{ for 8 months}$$

B. Stock Down—
Calls Expire

If BS is less than 30 the option will not be exercised. Any loss incurred owing to the sale of the stock will be determined by the difference between 29¼ plus commissions and the selling price of the stock less commissions. However, this loss would be mitigated by premiums and dividends received.

For example, if we sold our stock at 25 our loss would be calculated as follows:

Sales of 1,000 BS @ 25........		$25,000
Less commissions.............		(336)
Proceeds...................		$24,664
Cost 1,000 BS @ 29¼........	$29,250	
Plus commissions.............	363	
Capital loss*................		($ 4,949)

* The capital loss of $4,949 will be either short-term or long-term, depending on the holding period.

This capital loss of $4,949 would be offset by the $3,882 ($4,000 − $118) net premium received which would be viewed by the Internal Revenue Service as a capital gain plus the $800 dividend income received for a total of $4,682, thereby giving a pretax loss of $267. Naturally, each additional decline of one point in the stock would increase our loss by $1,000.

C. Stock Up—Unwind Position

Date	Action	Debit	Credit
June 1	Buy 1,000 BS @ 29¼ plus commissions........	$29,613	
June 1	Sell 10 calls BS @ 30 exp. 1/31/74 for $400 each......................................		$4,000
	Less commissions...........................		(118)

Let us assume that on July 31 we received a negative research report on BS (then trading at 32) and we wanted to sell our long stock and eliminate our call obligations:

```
We would sell 1,000
    BS @ 32...............          $32,000
Less commissions............            (380)
"Buy in" 10 calls BS
@ 30 exp. 1/31/74 for
    $450 each*.............  $4,500
Plus commissions...........    123
```

* This is an estimated price.

Return on Investment Calculation

```
Proceeds from sale of stock @ 32...        $31,620   ($32,000 − $380)
No dividends in this period.......             —
Original premiums received.......          3,882
                                         ───────
                                         $35,502

Cost of stock @ 29¼...........  $29,250
Plus commissions..............      363
Plus cost of "buy in" of calls.....   4,500
Plus commissions..............      123    $34,236
Pretax Profit.................             ───────
                                         $ 1,266
```

$$ROI = \frac{\text{Total pretax profit}}{\text{Investment}}$$

$$= \frac{\$1,266}{\$29,613 - \$3,882} = 4.9\% \text{ for 60 days}$$

D. Stock Down— Unwind Position

Date	Action	Debit	Credit
June 1	Buy 1,000 BS @ 29¼ plus commissions........	$29,613	
June 1	Sell 10 Calls BS @ 30 exp. 1/31/74 for $400 each..................................		$4,000
	Less commissions...........................		(118)

Let us assume that on July 31 we received a negative research report on BS (then trading at 28) and we wanted to sell our long stock and eliminate our call obligations:

```
We would sell 1,000 BS
    @ 28.....................          $28,000
Less commissions............              357
"Buy in" calls @ 30
exp. 1/31/74 for $250
    each*.....................  $2,500
Plus commissions............     105
```

* This is an estimated price.

Return on Investment Calculation

Proceeds from sale of stock @ 28...	$27,643	($28,000 − $357)
No dividends in this period........	—	
Original premiums received........	3,882	
	$31,525	
Cost of stock @ 29¼............. $29,250		
Plus commissions................ 363		
Plus cost of "buy in" of calls....... 2,500		
Pretax loss..................... 105	$32,218	
	($ 693)	

The important feature to be remembered about writing calls fully hedged is that the call premium affords downside protection for the stock owned, for the reason that the premium will be kept by the call writer if the stock remains at or below the strike price at the expiration date.

The reader, after studying the foregoing examples, may react by saying to himself "Why should I ever write calls fully hedged in a bull market? Why, I can easily pick a stock that will appreciate more than 18.2 percent in eight months!" This is a very common reaction, but the laws of probability don't seem to back the statement. The diagram on the preceding page (Figure 7–1) seems at first to support the idea that the buy stock strategy is the superior one. Above a five-point gain in price the buy stock strategy far outdistances the buy-stock–sell-call strategy. The key question is what prices are likely for the stock during the holding period? If a probability distribution based on a relevant history of a given stock's price behavior is superimposed on the diagram in Figure 7–1 an interesting comparison can be made. If the odds of achieving various price levels are used to estimate the overall profitability of the two strategies (see Figure 7–2), the buy-stock–sell-call will *always* have to outperform the buy stock strategy, given enough trials over time. The reason this is so is that the buy stock strategy loses as much as it gains for every point on either side of the breakeven level. The buy-stock–sell-call strategy, on the other hand, has a

FIGURE 7–1

Profit Comparison between Buying 100 Shares of Stock versus Buying the Stock and Writing a Call with a \$500 Premium

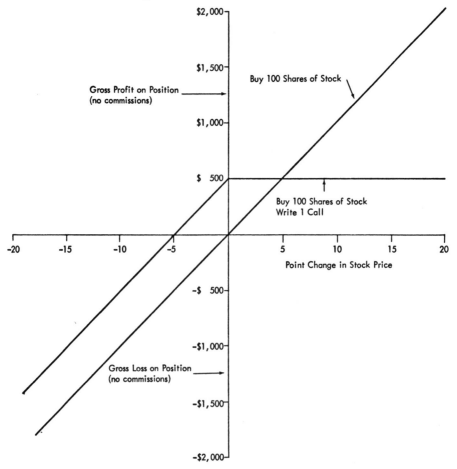

much smaller loss area than the buy stock strategy and a greater profit area in the relevant price range as well. In fact, no matter what the shape of the probability distribution, as long as it is symmetric around the price at which the position was established, the conclusion has to be the same. The only exception is the stock that totally changes its price characteristics over

FIGURE 7-2

Superimposing a Likely Distribution of Prices over the Profit Comparison between Buying 100 Shares of Stock versus Buying the Stock and Writing a Call with a $500 Premium

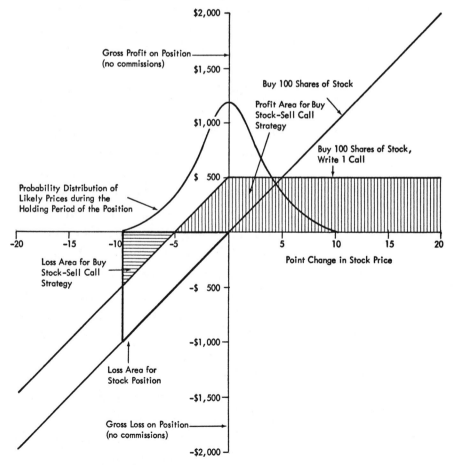

time. However, this is mainly true of young companies of small capitalization which suddenly become glamorized in Wall Street for some dramatic change in their fortunes. This situation is not typical of the giant behemoths traded on the CBOE which possess huge stock capitalizations, large trading volume, and the inability to so totally change the direction of the company in a short time span.

The relevant rules for buying stock and writing calls are:

1. Since the ideal environment for this strategy is a rising market, the strategy should be implemented in a bull market as defined by the market barometer.

2. The ideal time to establish such a position depends greatly on the objective the investor is attempting to achieve. If he desires a capital gain on his stock coupled with an ordinary loss on the call he is writing, his position should be established at the end of an intermediate decline in a bull market as defined in the price behavior chapter. If, instead, he prefers to write calls against a long-term holding which he prefers not to sell, the ideal time to write calls is at the end of an intermediate advance in a bull market so that the call premiums stand the greatest chance of being collected. If the call writer is so disposed and is working with stock that is so low priced that it will probably never be sold and thus never incur capital gains taxes, the investor has the

flexibility of writing calls at the end of intermediate rallies in both bull markets and bear markets. This is only true in this case because falling stock prices in a bear market are immaterial, the major objective being to collect call premiums. Where timing of establishing and closing of transactions is important, the timing tools presented in the chapter on high risk/high reward strategies should prove especially helpful.

3. In all cases it is desirable to write calls with premiums above fair value as determined by the pricing curves presented in the chapter on pricing. As a rule of thumb, premiums should be at least 25 percent greater than fair value.

The final strategy to be covered under the moderate risk/moderate reward category is the short-stock–sell-put strategy. This approach is ideally applied in a bear market in which the investor hopes to augment his short profits with the collection of put premiums, while at the same time affording himself the protection of the put premiums collected in case the stock is at or above the strike price at the expiration date. Again the medium of numerical examples will be used to demonstrate the four possible outcomes of this strategy. The Bethlehem Steel example just used for the buy-stock–write-call strategy will be adapted, assuming that the premiums used in those examples can now be thought of as put premiums.

A. Stock Is Up—
Position Closed
Out at a Loss

Date	Action	Debit	Credit
June 1	Short 1,000 BS @ 29¼...................		$29,250
	Less commissions.......................		($ 363)
June 1	Sell 10 puts BS @ 30, expiring Jan. 31, for		
	$400 each.............................		$ 4,000
	Less commissions.......................		($ 118)

On November 1, the stock is trading at 34 and the investor decides to close out his positions.

Buy 1,000 BS @ 34 plus commissions
  covering short........................ $34,389
Buy 10 puts BS @ 30, expiring Jan. 31,
  for $50 each.......................... $ 500
Plus commission....................... $ 50

Return on Investment Calculation

Proceeds..................................	$28,887	(29,250 − 363)
Plus premium.............................	3,882	(4,000 − 118)
	$32,769	
Less cost of stock..........................	($34,389)	(34,000 + 389)
Capital loss (short-term)....................	($ 1,620)	
Less closing cost of options.................	($ 550)	(500 + 50)
Total loss.................................	$ 2,170	

$$\text{ROI} = \frac{\text{Total pretax loss}}{\text{Investment}} = \frac{-2170}{25,005} \times 100$$
$$= -8.7\% \text{ for 5 months}$$

B. Stock Down—
Puts Exercised

Date	Action	Debit	Credit
June 1			
	Short 1,000 BS @ 29¼..................		$29,250)
	Less commissions.....................		($ 363)
June 1			
	Sell 10 puts BS @ 30, expiring January 31		
	for $400 each..		$ 4,000
	Less commissions.		($ 118)

The stock drops gradually to 25 at the expiration date and the put buyer elects to exercise his put by delivering his stock to the put writer (our investor) at a price of 30.

January 31

The put writer purchases 1,000 BS @ 30,
   honoring the puts he wrote............ $30,000
Plus commissions...................... $ 370

Return on Investment Calculation

Proceeds................................... $28,887   (29,250 − 363)
Plus premium..............................   3,882   (4,000 − 118)
                                          $32,769
Less cost of stock..........................($30,370)   (30,000 + 370)
Short-term capital gain.................... $ 2,399

$$\text{ROI} = \frac{\text{Total pretax gain}}{\text{Investment}} = \frac{2,399}{25,005} \times 100$$
$$= 9.6\% \text{ in 8 months}$$

C. Stock Down—
Position Closed Out

Date	Action	Debit	Credit
June 1			
	Short 1,000 BS @ 29¼.....................		$29,250
	Less commissions.........................		($ 363)
June 1			
	Sell 10 puts BS @ 30, expiring Jan. 31, for		
	$400 each..............................		$ 4,000
	Less commissions.........................		($ 118)

The stock drops sharply to 25 and the investor decides to close out his position.

August 1

Cover short of 1,000 shares BS @ 25...... $25,000
Plus commissions......... .. .. $ 336

August 1
Close out 10 puts BS @ 30 now trading
for $700 .... $ 7,000
Plus commissions .... $ 145

Return on Investment Calculation

Proceeds	$28,887	(29,250 − 363)
Plus premium	$ 3,882	(4,000 − 118)
	$32,769	
Less cost of stock	(25,336)	(25,000 + 336)
Less closing cost of puts	(7,145)	(7,000 + 145)
Profit	$ 288	

$$\text{ROI} = \frac{\text{Total pretax gain}}{\text{Investment}} = \frac{288}{25,005} \times 100$$
$$= 1.2\% \text{ in 2 months}$$

Actually, with this small a profit, the investor probably would not be tempted to unwind the position. If, instead, the profit approached the maximum of $2,399 he would receive as in case B with the puts being exercised, the incentive would then be greater, especially if this occurred early in the option's life.

D. The Stock Remains Virtually Unchanged

In this case the investor would simply collect the put premiums (less commissions) of $3,882 ($4,000 − $118) and probably write another put after the first one expired. In this case the return on investment would be

$$\frac{\text{Total pretax gain}}{\text{Investment}} = \frac{\$ 3,882}{\$25,005} \times 100$$
$$= 15.5\% \text{ in 8 months}$$

The short-stock–write-put strategy is very seldom employed, mainly because most option writers seem to be most comfortable with call writing fully hedged and attempt to do this regardless of the price environment they are in. In bull markets they make a lot of money and in bear markets they generally lose money. Their consolation may be that the premiums collected gave them a smaller loss than that suffered by someone who had simply purchased a stock, but the logical thing to do would have been to employ a bear market strategy.

The dynamics of the short-stock–write-put strategy are probably best demonstrated with the

FIGURE 7-3

Profit Comparison between Shorting 100 Shares of Stock versus Shorting the Stock and Writing a Put with a $500 Premium

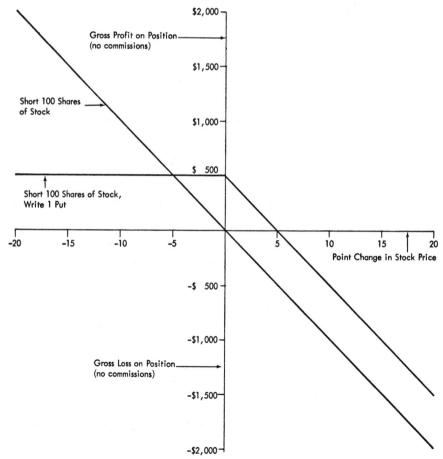

same type of diagram used for the buy-stock–write-call strategy. Figure 7–3 represents an example of a typical short-stock–write-put trade. This is compared with simply shorting stock. The profit profile of the put-writing strategy offers a maximum profit equal to the put premium for any price below the point where the position was established. Above that point the position loses ground at a rate of $100 per point of price increase until the point is reached at which the stock loss equals the put premiums (in our example, at a 5-point increase in the stock price). Again the relevant comparison with the short stock strategy is made by superimposing a probability distribution of likely prices. As with the call-writing example, an investor may ask why he should write a put, when he could make much more money simply shorting the stock. The answer is if one strives for consistently good results, the complement of a written put has to be superior for the large capitalization, cyclical stock traded on the CBOE. Otherwise, the investor is attempting the extreme case which is just not likely to occur. For the small capitalization company in extremis, that is another case entirely.

Another reason that call writers may tend to strictly write CBOE calls, when they have the alternative of puts, is that no dividends are received when writing puts. It may be painful to think of engaging in a policy which will not provide stock dividends, but the capital losses suffered in a bear market should more than make up for the difference.

Some rules that may be helpful in the short-stock–write-put strategy are the following:

1. Since the ideal environment for this strategy is a falling market, the strategy should be implemented in a bear market as defined by the market barometer.

2. The ideal time to implement the strategy is at the end of a rally in a bear market so that the chance of a move upwards against the position is at a minimum. For guidance, the methodology for recognizing such a point is covered in the chapter on price behavior. The time to close out positions is at the end of intermediate declines or through expiration if the strike price is far above the market price with only a month until maturity.

3. The objective should be to write puts with premiums at least 25 percent greater than fair value as measured with the pricing graphs in Chapter 3, using 80 percent of the fair value of a call as an estimate for the put.

In all the foregoing moderate reward/moderate risk strategies no mention has been made of the amount of capital to be used. A suggested procedure is to think of the two stock-trading strategies, shorting stock and buying calls, or buying stock and purchasing a put, as a gambling operation on a par with the buying of calls so that only risk capital is utilized which can be totally lost without affecting your life-style or the ability to pay bills. Of that capital, a fully invested position should be diversified among five different underlying stock positions without using margin. This approach, following the buying and selling techniques recommended, should keep the investor out of trouble, both financially and emotionally.

The two option-writing strategies can be thought of as a way to earn a higher return than with bonds, but with somewhat greater risk of eroding your principal. Therefore the recommended procedure for an overall money management approach would be to have well over half of total capital in a savings account, in quality government, corporate, and possibly municipal bonds, with the remainder dedicated to an option-writing strategy appropriate to the current price environment.

Each individual will have to determine which, if any, of the strategies presented in this book he would be most comfortable in attempting. This will be determined not only by the amount of personal means, but mainly by the temperament, interest, and time available for each individual. The conclusion may even be to select a professional to manage part of your capital. Even in this case the knowledge of the techniques presented in this book should prove helpful.

The Moderate Reward/ Minimal Risk Strategies

8

The strategies presented in this chapter should provide the major source of acceptance for CBOE options as an important money management tool. The reason for this is the simple truth that herein lies the key to consistently successful results in the stock market. No other strategies offer the same management of risk, while providing a very satisfactory return on invested capital. No other approach works as scientifically with the way stock prices truly behave. Rather than attempting to forecast a future price level, which no one has demonstrated publicly that he can do with any consistency, these strategies work with price ranges and the expected percent change in price which can reasonably occur during a specific time period. Such things can be measured at least in terms of probabilities and allowed for in the application of a strategy. Another relationship which can be well defined is the behavior of a particular CBOE option relative to its underlying stock. The best work in the field has been done by Fisher Black and Myron Scholes,[1] but

---

[1] F. Black and M. Scholes, "The Pricing of Options and Corporate Liabilities," *Journal of Political Economy*, vol. 81, no. 3, May/June 1973.

their mathematics is well above the heads of even the most astute Wall Street professionals. What they essentially did was to define the behavior of an arbitrage between stock purchased and call options in the same stock sold (written). This arbitrage concept is the heart of this chapter. Arbitrage is defined as the simultaneous purchase and sale of the same or equivalent security in order to profit from price discrepancies. Perhaps the best means of presenting the benefits of a stock-option arbitrage is to examine the graphs in Figures 8–1 and 8–2.

The first graph depicts the typical buy stock strategy, in this case for 100 shares of Upjohn. The prices shown actually occurred. The area covered by parallel lines represents the loss area for the stock, which begins below the purchase price of 93¼. There is only one direction for the price to move to realize a profit, up. This is the basic buy-and-keep-your-fingers-crossed strategy employed every day in the stock market, very often with little success.

The second graph presents the profit and loss picture for a partial hedge strategy. This position consists of 100 shares of Upjohn stock purchased at 93¼ a share, combined with the sale of three Upjohn July calls with a strike price of $100. The premium for each call is $1,350. Now, rather than there being a loss if the stock drops below 93¼, the stock has to drop *below* 52¾ to cause a loss or rise *above* 123⅝. In other words the position is protected above *and* below the price paid for the stock. The stock position is embedded in a profit zone. How does

FIGURE 8-1

Unprotected Stock Purchase

Purchase Date	Upjohn Market Price	Margin of Safety	Break-even Price	Maximum Profit
11/15/73	93¼	None	93¼	Unlimited

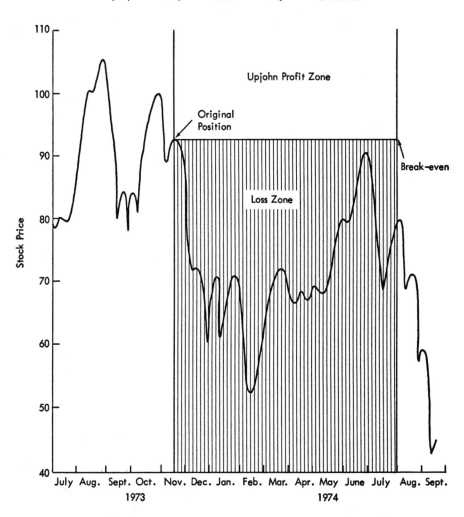

FIGURE 8–2

Partial Hedge Strategy

Date	Upjohn Market Price	Option Sold	Premium Received	Upper Protection	Lower Protection	Maximum Profit
11/15/73	93¼	July 100's	$1,350	123 5/8	52 3/4	89.5% in 8½ Months

Strategy { Sell 3 Upjohn Calls, July 100's @ $1,350 Each
Buy 100 Shares Upjohn @ 93¼

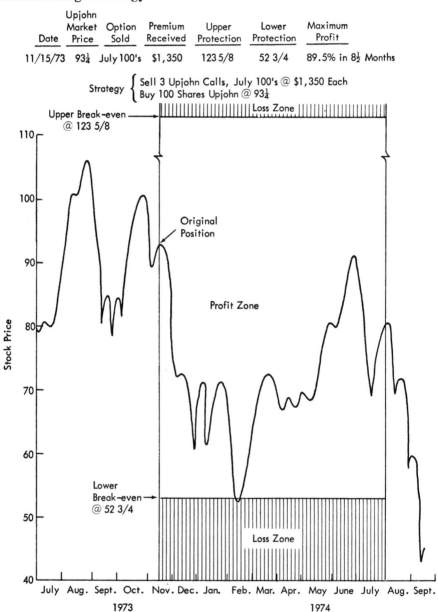

this occur? If the stock remains at or below the strike price of 100 at the expiration date, the call premiums will be collected. Since they would offset any decline in the stock's price, the lower breakeven is at the point where the loss in the stock's value equals the premiums collected. In this case the total premiums collected are $4,050 to be offset against 100 shares of stock, for a protection of $40\frac{1}{2}$ points.

The upper breakeven level is determined by a different means. As the stock rises in price the position gains on the increase in stock price but loses on the calls that are short until the point that the short loss overtakes the increase in the stock value plus the premiums collected. This is the upper breakeven level and can be determined both graphically and numerically, as we shall later see.

The key to understanding these arbitrage strategies lies in studying how option premiums change relative to the underlying stock, as well as the relationship between the strike price of the option and the current stock price, the volatility of the underlying stock price, the time remaining in the option's life, and the level of interest rates. Although this may appear to be a frightening array of relationships, it is possible to encapsulate them in a graph usually called the standard warrant diagram. Such diagrams are presented in Figures 8–3 to 8–7 for the five levels of volatility found in CBOE stocks.

In order to standardize the information as much as possible, the option premiums and stock prices are expressed as a ratio by dividing each

FIGURE 8–3. CBOE Analog of the Standard Warrant Diagram: Volatility—10 Percent

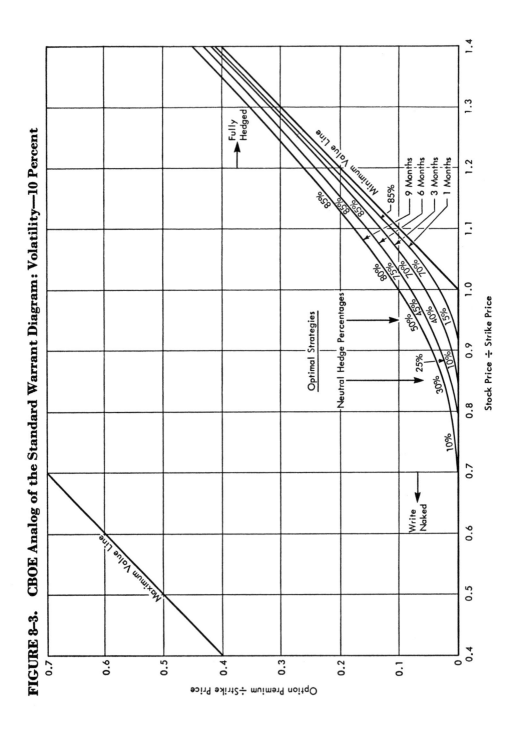

FIGURE 8–4. CBOE Analog of the Standard Warrant Diagram: Volatility—20 Percent

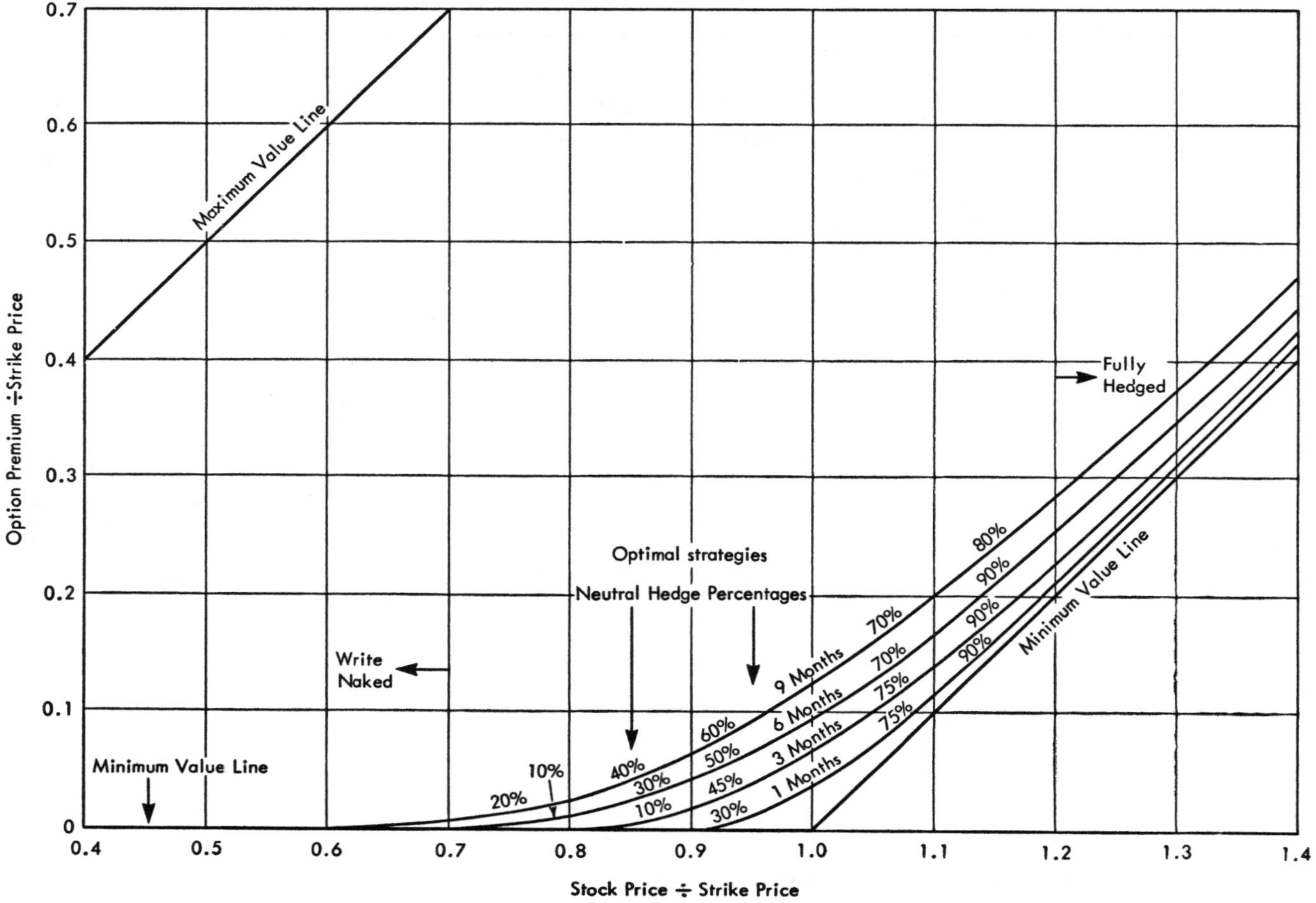

FIGURE 8–5. CBOE Analog of the Standard Warrant Diagram: Volatility—30 Percent

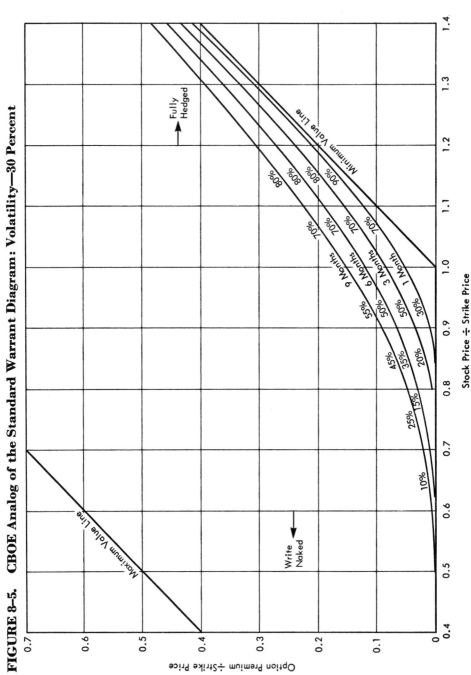

FIGURE 8-6. CBOE Analog of the Standard Warrant Diagram: Volatility—40 Percent

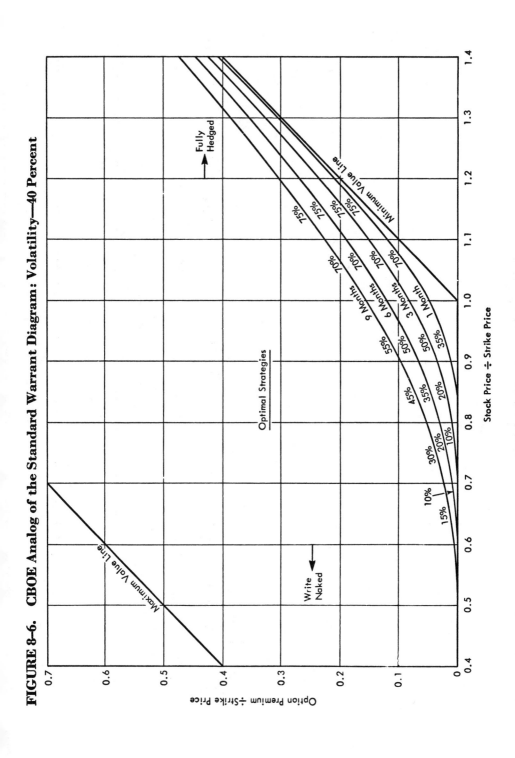

FIGURE 8-7. CBOE Analog of the Standard Warrant Diagram: Volatility—50 Percent

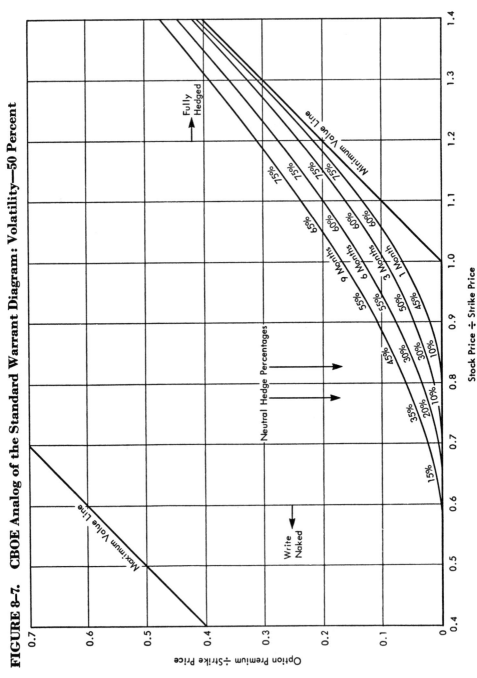

by the strike price of the option. If the stock price were trading exactly at the strike price of the option, the ratio would be 1.0 along the horizontal axis of the graph. The option premium expressed as a fraction of the option's strike price is plotted along the vertical axis. If an option had a premium of $1,000 and a strike price of 100, the ratio would be 0.1.

The values which an option premium can exhibit range between a theoretical maximum of equalling the price of the stock down to the cash value of the option at the expiration date. This minimum holds true because an option to buy 100 shares of stock at $100 a share is worth at least $500 less commission costs, if the stock is trading at $105 on the day the call options expire. Looking at the first standard warrant diagram, Figure 8–3, with 10-percent volatility, the maximum value line starts at a value of 0.4 and moves upward at a 45-degree angle so that at 0.5 on the option scale it corresponds with 0.5 on the stock scale. In actual practice option values tend to approximate the minimum value line, which runs along the bottom of the graph at a value of zero from readings of 0.4 on the stock price/strike price scale all the way up to 1.0. Above 1.0, the minimal value line begins to rise at a 45-degree angle so that each point equals the in-money value of the option. The price curves which relate the option premium to the underlying stock are derived from the premium curves presented in the chapter on the CBOE. Time on this diagram runs from the nine-month curve down to the minimum value line and demonstrates quite clearly the fact that a given option with the same strike price and underlying stock price as one with less time is worth more. For instance, on the 10-percent volatility graph at the stock price equals the strike price ratio 1.0, a nine-month option would have a premium of 0.1 of the strike price value of the stock ($1,000 if the strike price were $100), a six-month option would have a premium of $750, a three-month $500, and a one-month $250.

Actually the most important measurements which can be derived from the diagram are the degree of change in option premium for a point change in the underlying stock price and the upper and lower breakeven levels for any given ratio of options short in a position relative to stock owned. The slope of the various curves measures the degree of option premium change with a one-point change in the underlying stock. In the 10-percent volatility graph, Figure 8–3, the nine-month maturity line has an almost flat slope below a stock price/strike price ratio of 0.7, then gradually increases its slope until above a stock price/strike price ratio of 1.2, where the slope approaches a value of 1.0 or 45 degrees, equal to that of the minimum value line. In fact, the small numbers above the graph give the value of the slope over a narrow range starting at 10 percent and ranging up to 85 percent. We will come back to these important numbers in a short while. The second important measure, the upper and lower breakeven levels, is obtained by running a line from any given point on the curve upwards at the same slope as the curve at the starting point until the minimum value line is intersected above a value of 1.0. This is the upper breakeven level for the arbitrage being measured. Running the same line down to the left until it intersects the minimal value line running along the bottom of the graph below a level of stock price/strike price of 1.0 gives the lower breakeven level of any given arbitrage. As an example, let us suppose that a given nine-month option with 10-percent volatility has an option premium divided by a strike price of .075 and that the underlying stock is trading at $96 per share. As the example in Figure 8–8 shows, the slope of the price curve is 50 percent. What this means is that any movement in the underlying stock price near this point would shift the option premium by only half as much. Therefore, an arbitrage established with ten calls short, representing 1,000 shares of stock, and 500 shares of stock long would not change in value for small stock price changes around this point. If a line is drawn through this point with a slope of $\frac{1}{2}$ and extended upward to the upward sloping minimum value line, the value of the intersection is 1.2. This is where the position would be if it had a zero profit on the expiration date of the options. For our 100 strike price, this would translate into $120 a share for the stock. If the same line is extended downward to the left it hits the horizontal segment of the minimal value line at 0.82. This would be the value of the stock price which would also yield a zero profit at expira-

FIGURE 8-8

CBOE Analog of the Standard Warrant Diagram: Volatility—10 Percent

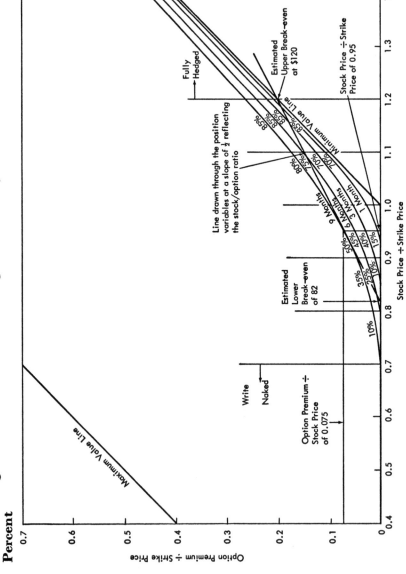

tion date and equals $82 in our case. Anywhere between $82 and $120 at the expiration date, the position will make a profit.

Perhaps the reader has a hint what this can mean for money management. The gist of it is that the standard diagram can be used to design an arbitrage position which will suffer no potential loss for small price moves away from the original stock price and will return a profit at expiration date within a 20-percent range above and below the current stock price. Since the price curves are relatively fixed, a position can be totally designed before it is established. If a range of 82 to 120 does not seem appropriate, the option/stock ratio can be adjusted so that a different set of breakeven levels results.

At this stage the next logical step in the explanation is to investigate how the upper and lower breakeven levels can be determined numerically and how the profit potential for each position can be determined as well. The simplest and yet most versatile means of determining the upper and lower breakeven levels is with "tee" account analysis. Such bookkeeping entries are identical to the entries made for various transactions in the monthly account statement provided by most brokerage firms.

Let's use our example of a stock with a price of $96 a share, let us call it XYZ Corp., and have a nine-month call option with a strike price of $100 trading at $750 each. If our standard curves indicate an ideal position of ten calls short and 500 shares of stock long, our T-account entries would be as follows:

1. Purchase 500 shares of XYZ Corp. at 96 for 500 × $96 or $48,000. The entry would be:

Debit	Credit
1. $48,000	

2. Sell 10 XYZ call options maturing in nine months for $750 each for a positive cash flow in the account of $7,500. The entry would be:

Debit	Credit
1. $48,000	2. $7,500

3. By selling ten calls, the writer is now obligated to deliver 1,000 shares of XYZ Corp. stock at a price of $100 to honor the calls, or a total obligation of $100,000. The entry to reflect this is:

Debit	Credit
1. $48,000	2. $ 7,500
	3. 100,000

Netting out the account, the investor finds himself with a net credit of $59,500.

Debit	Credit
1. $48,000	2. $ 7,500
	3. 100,000
	$107,500
	−48,000
	$ 59,500

This amount is the extent of the open obligation the investor has by owning only 500 shares of XYZ Corp. stock to honor a 1,000-share obligation at $100 a share. If the 500 shares he is net short were to be acquired for $59,500, the deficit in the account, the overall position would break even. By dividing the $59,500 by 500 shares, the result of $119 a share is obtained as the breakeven price. This compares with our graphical estimate of $120.

If the stock price remains at or below $100 a share at the expiration date, the obligation to deliver 1,000 shares of XYZ Corp. at $100 is removed. The T-account would look like this:

Debit	Credit
1. $48,000	2. $ 7,500
	3. ~~$100,000~~

or,

Debit	Credit
1. 48,000	2. $ 7,500

Since the premiums will be kept at or below $100, the $7,500 acts as an offset against any loss in the 500 shares of stock purchased at 96. The figure of $48,000 minus $7,500, or $40,-500, could be attained for the stock and the position would break even. The amount $40,500 divided by 500 equals $81, providing the lower breakeven price. Another way to arrive at the same number is to divide the premiums collected by 500 shares, or $7,500 divided by 500 shares, for 15 points of protection. Subtracting this from 96 yields the lower breakeven of $81.

The reason for introducing the tee account approach is that it is the most general and easily adaptable to complex positions. If stock is purchased at many different prices, the total dollar value would still appear on the left-hand side of the tee account. The total premiums would appear in the right-hand side along with the total dollar value of the delivery obligation of all the calls that are short. The upper breakeven point would still be obtained by netting out the overall position and dividing the difference between the left-hand and the right-hand sides by the net amount of stock short in the position. The lower breakeven would be determined by dividing the number of shares in the long position into the total premium income possible and obtaining the points of protection for the position. Subtracting this number from the average cost per share of the long position provides the lower breakeven level.

Computing the maximum profit level for the position is the other important variable to determine. The maximum profit level is attained at the strike price of the short options in the position. This occurs because at this point the best price possible is obtained for the long stock, while one still collects all the premiums written. Therefore to compute the maximum profit possible one simply adds the profits gained by the long stock's moving up to the strike price to the dollar value of the premiums collected. In our case this would be 500 shares times (100 −

96) = 4 or $2,000 plus the total premium income of $7,500 for a grand total of $9,500. To compute this as a return on capital simply divide this number by the dollars needed to purchase the long stock less the premiums on the

FIGURE 8-9

The Profit Profile

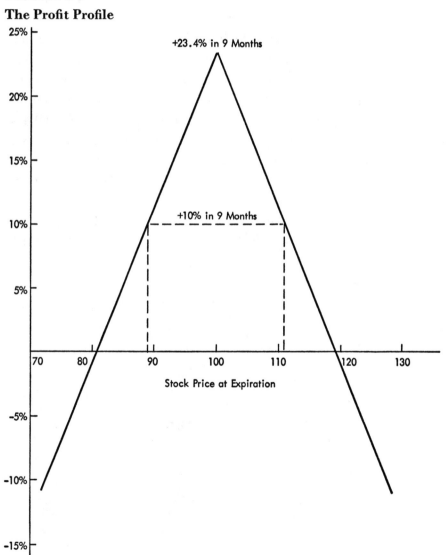

Stock Price at Expiration

short calls. In our case this would be $48,000 less $7,500 and divided into $9,500 would yield a 23.4 percent pretax return for nine months.

The profit profile for the arbitrage thus assumes the shape of a triangle as shown in Figure 8–9, with the apex at the strike price of 100. Interestingly, even if the stock closes as low as 90 or as high as 112 at the expiration date, the return on capital is 10 percent in nine months. Not a bad target for a medium as imprecise as the stock market. If this were a more complex position one could perform the same analysis using the weighted average strike price for all the options in the position along with the tee account method for computing the breakeven levels.

The flexibility of designing the hedge position can probably be best appreciated by computing a range of breakeven levels for our XYZ Corp. position for a full range of hedge values. Table 8–1 presents this analysis with the percent hedge

TABLE 8–1

Hedge (percent)	Upper Breakeven	Lower Breakeven
0	107½	Profit of $7,500
10	108¾	21
20	110⅜	58½
30	112⅜	71
40	115⅛	77¼
50	119	81
60	124¾	83½
70	134¼	85¼
80	153½	86⅝
90	211	87⅝
100	00	88½

convention indicating how much stock is owned relative to the short options in the position. The incredible result is that the position can be made to realize a profit for a stock price ranging from zero to infinity. Of course the catch is that if an extreme position had to be properly adjusted by either totally covering the outstanding calls to protect a large price rise, or writing enough calls to buy enough downside protection a near infinite amount of funds would be required. Nonetheless, the degree of flexibility is amazing.

Now that virtually all the parameters have been covered, how does one go about designing a position? The first question to answer is, which option should I write? The answer is obtained by scanning the available option premiums, preferably with large premiums in terms of fair value. A good "write" as it is called would be two- to four-month options with premiums at least 25 percent above fair value as determined by the pricing curves in the chapter on pricing. Also to be considered is the nature of the fundamentals of the underlying stock. A stable company with solid fundamentals should be the candidate. The next question is how much of a hedge to establish. This is estimated roughly by entering the appropriate standard curve for the correct level of volatility and the current premium level and stock price combination. The recommended hedge is provided by the numbers on the curve closest to the point determined by the option premium and stock price. With this as a guide, the next question is, how much protection do I need? To provide this answer, a set of curves was generated, Figures 8–10 and 8–11, which portray the largest percentage down moves recorded for the ten years through June 30, 1974, for the different levels of volatility

FIGURE 8–10

Volatility versus Maximum Percentage Up Moves

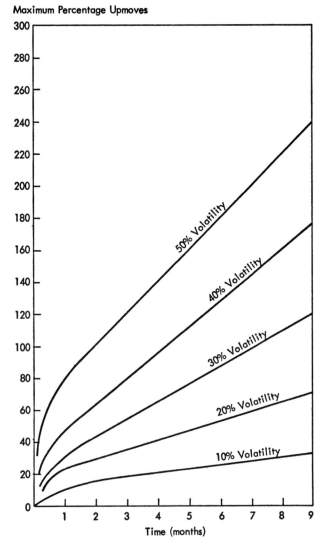

Maximum Percentage Upmoves

Time (months)

FIGURE 8–11

Volatility versus Maximum Percentage Down Moves

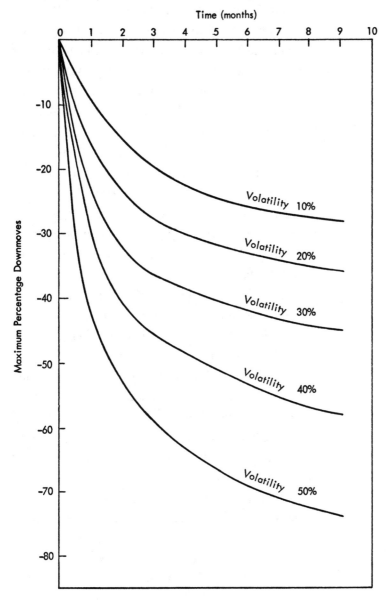

found on the CBOE. Since these curves give the maximum percent increases or decreases, they should yield safe breakeven levels. Once the breakeven level protection has been determined from these graphs, the percent hedge can be modified away from the neutral posture recommended with the standard curves. It is these breakeven levels which should determine the percent hedge. This can probably best be estimated by use of a ruler to test various sloped lines through a position point on the standard curve until the desired breakeven levels have been attained. This approximate slope, whether $\frac{1}{5}$, $\frac{1}{4}$, or whatever it may be, can be used to compute the actual breakevens using the tee account analysis for the final check. In case it is not possible to bracket both levels with a given hedge percentage, the upper breakeven should determine the hedge in a bear market.

The other cross check should be a computation of the maximum percent return, with a suggested cutoff of a minimum 40 percent annual pretax return on invested capital. The next step is to establish five to ten equally sized positions. A time period of two to four months is suggested because the breakeven levels are reasonable. Beyond this time period, the span of the breakeven levels would have to be too wide to allow for the maximum expected range in the underlying stock's price.

How should the positions be managed? The simplistic approach is to establish the widest breakeven limits possible and just allow the position to remain unadjusted for the life of the options. The risk is that occasionally one of the breakeven levels will be threatened and the level can then be either adjusted further away, or the position closed out. Another approach, which is preferred by the computer-oriented investors, is to establish filter levels, such as every 5 percent change in the underlying stock, where another 100 shares of stock is purchased if the stock is rising in price or another call is written if the stock is falling in price. In general, the most effective way to manage the positions is with a day-to-day monitoring of each position by tracking the price level of the underlying stock, the changes in the premium levels and the up-to-date profit and loss for both the stock and option sides of the arbitrage. The most sensible management of money comes from making small adjustments in response to day-to-day changes in the market. If the market begins to weaken, all breakeven levels should be reviewed to see whether more downside protection is needed. If the full protection dictated by the maximum price change curves was not initially set up, the position can be adjusted to a point near or actually encompassing this extreme level. This is the art of the method. Experience will teach how much to adjust, but several guidelines can be followed to aid in the decision making process.

1. The maximum profit attainable for each hedge position should be computed so that the position can be closed out in case this level is approximated before the options expire.

2. Any adjustments made in the hedges should be accomplished by either buying more stock or writing more calls, rather than taking losses by selling out stock to increase the ratio of calls to stock, or buying back calls at a loss to increase the percent hedge.

3. When establishing a position one should take a moderate posture, usually ranging from a 30-percent to a 60-percent hedge. In this way severe adjustments are avoided in case the stock changes direction radically. It is recommended that 30 percent of available funds be invested in 90-day treasury bills in case added buying power is needed to purchase stock for adjustment purposes.

4. The philosophy of the partial hedge should be to attempt to let the options expire with the stock price as close to the maximum profit level as possible, providing enough breakeven level protection so that the risk of a loss is kept to a minimum, and capitalizing on any profit opportunities which arise from unexpected price changes.

5. The only way that market judgment is used is to recognize when an extreme move has occurred in the market and take the resulting profits, while moderating any extreme postures which could be hurt by a sharp reversal of prices.

For bear market arbitrageurs, there is the short-stock–write-put variation of the partial hedge strategy. The standard warrant diagrams on the following pages show the neutral hedge percentages for various volatility stocks and permit the same design steps detailed under the long-stock–write-call discussion. The major difference lies in the computation of the upper and lower breakeven levels. The simplest case is for the upper breakeven level. If we again use our XYZ Corporation example, for this case we will short 100 shares of the stock at 96, creating a credit of $48,000. If we write ten XYZ 100 puts, with a premium of 11, we create a credit of $11,000, and the following tee account:

Debit	Credit
~~$100,000~~	$48,000
	$11,000
	$59,000

At the upper breakeven level, the 10 puts will not be exercised, thus eliminating a potential debit of $100,000, shown crossed out in the tee account. Breakeven would be for a purchase of 500 shares of stock, covering short for $59,000 or $118 a share.

The lower breakeven would use the same tee account above, in this case having to honor the exercise of 10 puts at a price of $100 a share. If the 500 shares not presently short were sold short for the difference of $100,000 minus $59,000, or $41,000, this would amount to a price of 82.

To operate the strategy, many of the same guidelines should be used as for the buy-stock–write-calls partial hedge. Five to ten equal dollar-size positions should be established with an ideal pretax annual profit potential of 40 percent. Options with two to four months life should be used because the breakeven levels can closely bracket the maximum savings expected. This can be a serious problem when operating in a bear market, because large price drops occur during very short periods of time. The necessary capital should be available to become fully hedged in all positions. In fact, these positions can not be forgotten until expiration day. Daily profit and loss statements should be kept to allow very close monitoring and adjustment. Small adjustments should be made either writing more puts if the stock rallies, or shorting more stock if the stock drops.

Some important guidelines for operating the strategy follow:

1. The maximum profit attainable for each hedge position should be computed so that the position can be closed out in case this level is approximated before the options expire. This is where the profit and loss marking to the market is so important.
2. Any adjustments made in the hedges should be accomplished by either shorting more stock or writing more puts, rather than taking losses by covering shorts or buying back puts at a loss.
3. When establishing a position, one should take a moderate posture, meaning a 30- to 60-percent hedge. Usually slightly out of the money puts will be used, since this is where premiums are the most overvalued. It

is recommended that 30 percent of available funds be invested in 90-day Treasury Bills in case added purchasing power is needed for adjustment.

4. The philosophy of any partial hedge is to attempt to let the options expire with the stocks as close to the maximum profit level as possible. If only one strike price put is used, this would mean expiring at the strike price. The breakeven levels provide a profit cushion against modest price changes. Any unexpected price changes which create a profit opportunity should be taken advantage of.

5. The only way that market judgment is used is to recognize when an extreme move has occurred in the market and take the resulting profits. If an extreme reversal would cause great losses, such as at the top of a bear market rally with a large ratio of puts written, the position should be brought back to a more balanced posture.

While the partial hedge approach just discussed attempts to capture the maximum profits available from an arbitrage between short stock and short puts, the neutral hedge is a variation which attempts to capture overvalued call premiums without managing breakeven levels or closing out positions at market turns. The essence of the neutral hedge is to have no feeling whatsoever of future price directions. The mechanics of the method are to search for overvalued premiums as determined by the option

FIGURE 8–12
Put Option Analog of the Standard Warrant Diagram: Volatility—50 Percent

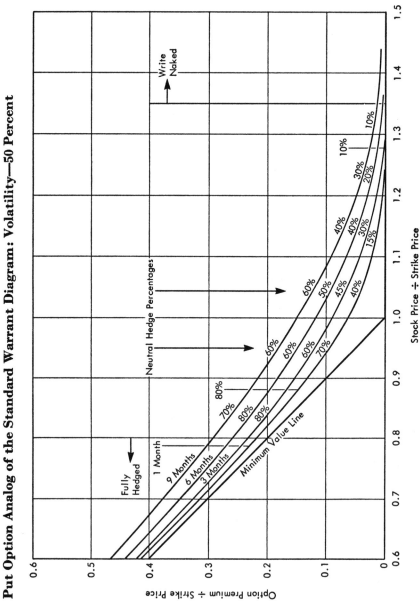

FIGURE 8-13
Put Option Analog of the Standard Warrant Diagram: Volatility—40 Percent

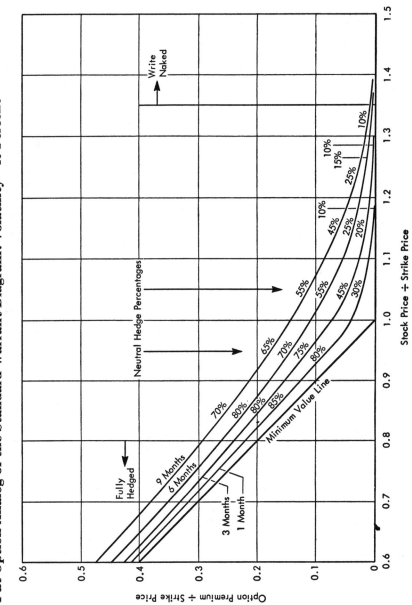

FIGURE 8-14
Put Option Analog of the Standard Warrant Diagram: Volatility—30 Percent

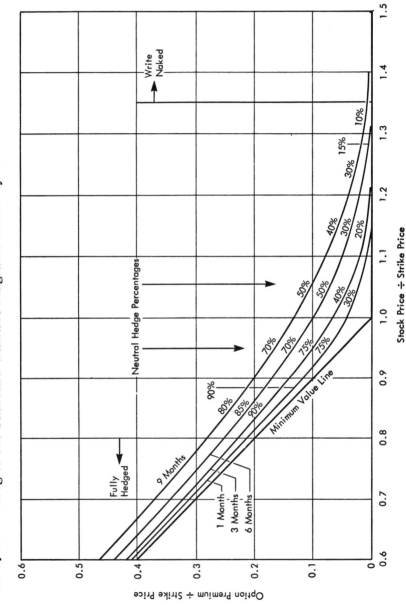

FIGURE 8–15

Put Option Analog of the Standard Warrant Diagram: Volatility—20 Percent

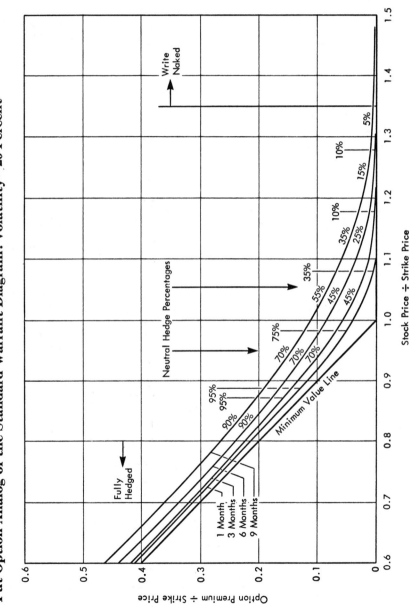

FIGURE 8-16
Put Option Analog of the Standard Warrant Diagram: Volatility—10 Percent

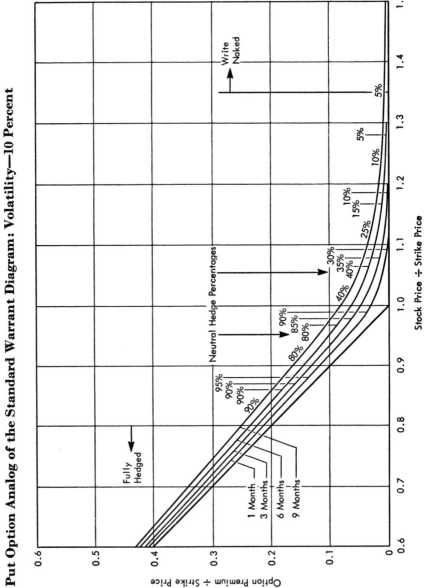

pricing curves of Chapter 3. The initial percent hedge established is determined by entering the standard warrant diagram and reading the recommended percent hedge from the curves. Once this hedge is established it is adjusted only as dictated by the percentages on the curve. If a 30-percent hedge was the initial position—for example, 300 shares of stock purchased and 10 calls sold—and the slope on the curves called for a 40-percent hedge, another 100 shares of stock would be purchased. If the curves called for a 20-percent hedge, 100 shares of stock would be sold. Because so much adjusting is required, the guideline of always adding to a position to adjust as in the partial hedge has to be ignored, for otherwise the position would become too large for the available capital. As the stock moves higher in price a fatter hedge is called for, which means selling some calls, usually at a loss. If the stock price moves lower a smaller hedge is called for, which means selling some stock, usually at a loss. Over time, the process tends to yield a profit as overvalued calls become less overvalued and are therefore closed out at a gain in the constant adjustment process.

As one might imagine, this strategy, while requiring no market judgment whatsoever, demands constant monitoring to the point of watching prices sometimes from minute to minute. The costs of the transactions (brokerage commissions, fees, and taxes) are prohibitive, which relegates this approach to a member of the CBOE or other appropriate options exchange.

A somewhat less flexible approach than the partial hedge, but requiring far less capital, is a technique called spreading. Essentially the method is to buy a call as a substitute for purchasing stock in an arbitrage. There are many variations on this basic theme, but one very sensible one will be presented. The procedure is to look for a pair of options in a given underlying stock that have the same expiration dates, but different strike prices, where the premium of the lower strike price option is twice that of the higher strike price option. An actual example which existed in April 1974 with Atlantic Richfield calls, were the October 90s trading at $600 and the October 100s trading at $337.50. The recommended hedge is 33 percent for several reasons, the first one being a positive cash flow for the position. The three calls sold would provide $1,012.50 in premiums deposited in the account, while the call purchased would cause a cash drain of $600. This net cash flow is important because, if the stock remained at or below 100 until the expiration date, that amount of $1,012.50 minus $600, or $412.50, would be the gross profit for the position. In fact, even if the stock dropped to zero, this amount would be the gross profit for the position. There is no downside risk. If the options were to expire with the stock above 90, the long option would be worth the in-money value or $100 for each point above 90. The maximum profit in the position would be attained at a price of 100, at which the investor would enjoy $1,000 for his one long call and collect $1,012.50 in premiums for his short calls. This total of $2,012.50 less the cost of the long call, $600, would yield a profit of $1,412.50. Above a price of 100, the position would begin eroding by $200 per point rise because of the 200 shares net short in the option position. The gross profit of $1,412.50 would finally be overcome if the stock rose above $107\frac{1}{8}$. This is the upper breakeven point. Since the stock at the time of the trade was 86, the position had unlimited downside protection and 21 points' protection on the upside. The actual margin requirements for the trade, using New York Stock Exchange rules were as follows:

1. Purchase one call October Atlantic Richfield 90 for $600. Cash required $600.
2. Sell three calls October Atlantic Richfield 100s for $3\frac{3}{8}$ each. The margin requirement for each call is:
   a. Thirty percent of the market value of the stock $= 0.3 \times \$8,600 = \$2,580$.
   b. Less the premium of the option sold, or $337.50, reducing the $2,580 to $2,242.50.
   c. Less the mark to the market of the short call, or $100 - 86 = \$1,400$, further reducing the margin requirement to $842.50. For the three calls this amounts to $2,527.50.[2]

---

[2] New uniform margin rules in effect after February 1975 would only require $1,957.50. See Chapter 9 for a further explanation.

Therefore total cash required in the account is $2,527.50 + $600, or $3,127.50, if no marginable stock is available to cover the three short calls. For this, there is an opportunity to make $1,412.50 in six months for a 45.2 percent pretax return on capital.

There are many ways to handle the spread position. The simplest approach is to remain with the position until the options expire, closing it out if the position reaches a predetermined loss prior to expiration. The predetermined loss should be less than 20 percent of the margin required for the hedge. The more active approach involves market timing and judgment in line with the work in the chapter on trading techniques. In this case the spread is established at a perceived market turn. If an expected rally occurs, the spread trader "lifts the leg" and closes out the protective short call, thus converting the spread into a long call trade. This should only be done at the end of intermediate declines in a bull market and with options having at least two months of life. The beauty of the method is there is no downside risk if it is done correctly, allowing the trader to establish his position on weakness, yet protect himself from being early.

The opposite approach to trading with spreads is to establish a position at the end of a rally in a bear market. Upon receipt of evidence that the expected decline is beginning, the long call leg is closed out and the short call allowed to ride with the decline. In this manner the short trade is given a large amount of upside protection in case the trade is established early, yet allows the trader to attempt a high price level for his short call. The variations are nearly infinite. However, the true benefit of spreading is the large flexibility in strategies and maneuverability that can be obtained for a small amount of capital. For the aspiring option investor this is undoubtedly the best and safest training ground.

Spreading

9

There is a dream in options investing to find a strategy with a sure profit. And *spreading* is the domain for that quest. A whole new vocabulary has been invented: butterflies, calendars, verticals, horizontals. The permutations and combinations boggle the mind. The danger is that the complexity of these strategies can lead to the self-delusion that they can somehow produce sure profits. Worse yet, it is an area where brokers can lose a client's understanding as well as his money. What this chapter will attempt to do is to describe the more popular and sensible strategies, with some guidelines as to how to make each strategy most successful.

First of all, what is a spread? It is simply a hedged position in the options of a given underlying stock, where part of the position will appreciate with a given change in the underlying stock price, while the remainder of the position will depreciate. For example, with an underlying stock at a price of 50, an option strategist might purchase a 50 strike price call and sell a 40 strike call with the same maturity. If the stock drops in price, the deep-in-the-money 40 call sold will appreciate at a greater rate than the 50 strike option loses. This is a bearish call spread. The selection of the appropriate options depends heavily on the standard warrant diagrams presented in Chapter 8. One has to know the degree of price movement produced in each spread component based on a given change in the underlying stock.

As an aid to understanding, the spread strategies will be presented according to whether the outlook is a large up move in the underlying stock, a large down move, for either a large up or large down move, or for the stock to remain virtually unchanged. To further assist in the explanation, some special matrices will be presented, which were inspired by Humphrey E. D. Lloyd's book, *Spread Trading in Listed Options.*[1]

BULLISH
STRATEGIES

Vertical Spread
with Calls

The first strategies we will investigate are those for profiting from a ten-percent or greater rise in the underlying stock. Our first candidate is a bullish vertical spread with calls. The strategy can be diagrammed as follows:

Position Diagram

←——— TIME ———→

S	Calls		Near	Mid	Far
T	Out of the money			Sell	
R	At the money				
I	In the money			Buy	
K					
E					

---

[1] Humphrey E. D. Lloyd, *Spread Trading in Listed Options,* Windsor Books, P.O. Box 280, Brightwaters, N.Y. 11718.

Example

Stock......................	Texas Instruments
Date.......................	April 1
Stock Price.................	85
Short call..................	July 90 @ 2½
Long call..................	July 80 @ 7¾
Basis	7¾ − 2½ = $525

Principle. The principle of this strategy is to purchase an in-the-money call with at least two to three months of life remaining, which will follow the price movement of the underlying stock at a 70-percent or greater rate of change (a delta of more than 70 percent). This long call is hedged with an out-of-the-money short call which has a delta of 40 percent or less. The purpose is to enjoy a greater profit on the long call than is lost on the short call if a sizable rally of more than 10 percent occurs in the underlying stock.

Ideal Price Environment. Since this strategy needs a positive price environment to be successful it should be used only when the market barometer indicates a market dominated by uptrends. Except for the first 7 to 11 months of a new bull market, when rallies last longer and move farther than expected, most profits are usually taken after two to five weeks. The trend-measuring techniques presented in the chapter on price behavior should be used to time the placing of the position and the unwinding of it. Success should also be greater if the intermediate cycle measure has also just given a buy signal.

Tactics. The ideal circumstances for this spread are as small a basis as possible, the basis being the difference between the cost of the long in-the-money call less the premium received for the short out-of-the-money call. In our Texas Instruments example this is $7\frac{3}{4}$ less $2\frac{1}{2}$, or $525. When entering an order for such a spread, a limit should be set at the current market basis, if this is attractive, using the term *debit* after the $5\frac{1}{4}$ basis. This tells the floor broker you are looking for that basis or less as your goal. As an aid in determining an attractive basis, it should be compared to the potential profit of the spread. As a rule of thumb, if the stock moves 10 percent in four weeks, the profit before commissions should be greater than 50 percent of the basis. If not, the potential reward is simply not great enough.

Profit Profile. The maximum profit for this spread is the difference in the strike prices of the two options less the basis. In our Texas Instru-

FIGURE 9-1

Profit Profile (4 weeks later)

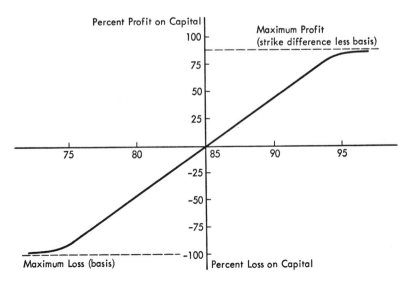

ments case, this is $1,000 minus $525, or $475, less commissions. The maximum loss is the basis plus commissions. As the profit graph Figure 9–1 indicates, the slope above and below the breakeven line is very similar, indicating that unless there is a bias in the market toward higher prices there is a 50/50 chance of a profit. In this case the maximum loss is greater than the maximum gain, which is also not ideal. If one uses the benchmarks of an adequate return on capital of 50 percent on a 10-percent price change, plus a maximum gain greater than the maximum loss, there will be few good bull spreads found. However, this type of selectivity goes a long way toward ensuring success.

The next strategy for a large price up move is a bullish spread with puts. The grid diagram is presented below:

Bullish Spread with Puts

		← TIME →		
S	*Puts*	*Near*	*Mid*	*Far*
T	In the money		Sell	
R	At the money			
I	Out of the money		Buy	
K				
E				

Example

Stock........................	Eastman Kodak
Date........................	June 3
Stock price....................	64
Short put.....................	Oct 70 @ 7
Long put.....................	Oct 60 @ 1¼
Basis........................	$7 - 1\frac{1}{4} = \$575$

Principle. The principle of this spread is to sell an in-the-money put, which will lose its premium at a greater rate than the long out-of-the-money put with which it is paired. The in-the-money put should enjoy a delta of 70 or greater, while the out-of-the-money put should have a delta of 40 or less. As in the case of the bullish call spread, the options should have a life of at least two to three months.

Ideal Price Environment. Again the price climate should favor rising stock prices, meaning a market barometer composition dominated by stocks in uptrends. To enhance success, the timing techniques for individual stocks presented in the price behavior chapter should be used for the opening and closing out of positions. Buying should be done when the intermediate cycle measure has also just given a buy.

Tactics. The goal of this spread is to obtain as large a basis as possible, which in the case of our Eastman Kodak spread is $700 minus $125, or $575. When entering an order for this spread, a quote should be obtained for the current basis, and if this is satisfactory, the order should be placed with a limit of this basis with the term *credit* added meaning you would prefer an even higher basis if possible. The basis should be deemed attractive if a 10-percent rally in the underlying stock during four weeks would yield a profit before commissions of greater than 50 percent of the basis. This estimate can be obtained from the premium evaluation graphs in the Chapter on pricing options.

Profit Profile. The maximum profit of this spread is the spread basis less commissions, the maximum loss is the difference in strike prices less the basis, naturally plus commissions. For our Kodak example, this would be a maximum profit of $575 before commissions and a maximum loss of $1,000 minus $575, or $425 plus commissions.

The profit/loss graph Figure 9–2 is similar to that of a bullish call spread in that the profit profile is fairly symmetric above and below the stock price where the position was opened. The same comment holds true that a 50/50 chance of a profit exists unless there is a general bias in the stock market toward higher prices. The profit guidelines of a potential gain of 50 percent of capital on a 10-percent rise in the underlying stock plus a larger maximum gain than the maximum loss should be strictly adhered to.

A few comments regarding the above two strategies should be mentioned. Since these bull-

FIGURE 9–2

Profit Profile (4 weeks later)

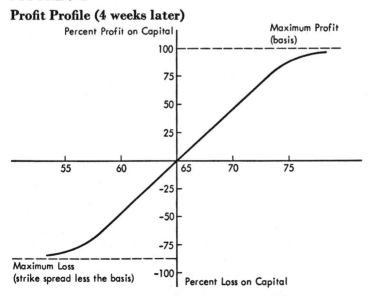

ish spreads are based on the likelihood of a significant short-term rise in the price of an underlying stock, an outright purchase of a call option should prove superior. The maximum loss would be similar, but more importantly, the potential for a gain of more than 50 percent on the capital committed is a far greater likelihood. Better yet, the commission costs for a completed trade should be roughly half that of the spread positions.

BEARISH STRATEGIES
Vertical Spread Using Calls

The aim of the following bearish strategies is to capitalize on a drop of at least 10 percent in an underlying security. The first strategy is a bearish vertical spread using calls. The spread diagram below indicates that the bearish position is accomplished by selling an in-the-money mid-term call with a delta of at least 70 percent. The short call is hedged by purchasing an out-

		←———	TIME	——→	
S		*Calls*	Near	Mid	Far
T	90	Out of the money		Buy	
R		At the money			
I	80	In the money		Sell	
K					
E					

Example

Stock.....................	Texas Instruments
Date......................	April 1
Stock price.................	85
Short call..................	July 80 @ 7¾
Long call..................	July 90 @ 2½
Basis.....................	7¾ − 2½ = $525

of-the-money mid-term call with a delta of less than 40 percent. The purpose is to enjoy a larger degree of price deterioration with the in-the-money call than is lost on the deterioration of the long out-of-the-money call.

Ideal Price Environment. As this strategy depends for its success on a 10-percent or greater drop in the underlying stock during the life of the calls, a generally deteriorating market is required. For this reason, the strategy should only be employed with market barometer readings indicating a market dominated by downtrends.

The trend-measuring techniques covered in the price behavior chapter should be used to establish and unwind the position. Success should be enhanced if the intermediate cycle measure has just given a sell signal.

Tactics. The ideal spread conditions are as large a basis as possible as this is the maximum profit potential. The basis in the case of our example is the premium received for the short call less the cost of the long call, this being 7¾ minus 2½, or $525! If the current market basis is attractive an order should be entered for the spread with this basis, with the term *credit* added to instruct the floor broker to obtain a spread at least as great as your limit. Again, some profit guidelines should be helpful. If the underlying stock drops 10 percent in four weeks, the profit before commissions should be greater than 50 percent of the basis.

Profit Profile. The maximum profit for the vertical bear spread with calls is the basis just discussed, or $525 less commissions. The maxi-

FIGURE 9–3

Profit Profile (4 weeks later)

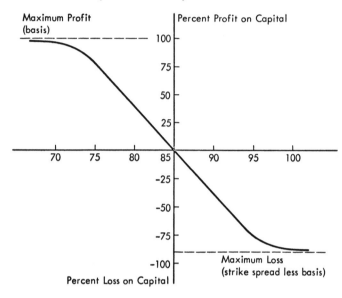

mum loss is the difference in strike prices less
the basis. In our Texas Instruments case, this
amounts to 90 minus 80, or 10 points less the
basis of $525, or $475 plus commissions.

The profit diagram Figure 9–3 indicates that
the rate of profit gain above the breakeven line
is virtually identical to the rate of loss decline
below. As with the bull spreads, unless there is
a probability bias toward lower prices, there is
a 50/50 chance of a profit. For our Texas Instruments bear spread the maximum gain is
greater than the maximum loss, which is good.
The final and perhaps most important criterion
to be met is a potential return on capital, the
capital being the minimum margin requirement
in this case of $475, of at least 50 percent

produced by a 10-percent drop in the underlying stock.

The alternative bearish spread strategy is a
vertical bearish spread with puts, which can
be diagrammed as follows:

Vertical Spread
with Puts

S		Puts	Near	Mid	Far
T	260	In the money		Buy	
R	250	At the money			
I	240	Out of the money		Sell	
K					
E					

←—— TIME ——→

Example

Stock	IBM
Date	June 3
Stock price	250
Short put	Oct. 240 @ 5
Long put	Oct. 260 @ 16
Basis	16 − 5 = 11

Principle. The principle of this strategy is to
buy an in-the-money put, where the strike price
is above the current market price and hedge that
purchase by selling an out-of-the-money put. If
the underlying stock drops in price, the in-the-
money put will appreciate at a faster rate than
the out-of-the-money. In other words, you would
gain at a greater rate on the long side of the
spread than would be lost by the short side of
the spread.

The ideal parameters are to select an in-the-money put with a delta of greater than 70 percent and an out-of-the-money put with a delta of less than 40 percent.

In order for this spread to be attractive, a potential drop in price of 10 percent over a four- to six-week period should be considered likely. The market environment should favor such a drop, therefore requiring the market barometer to be indicating a stock market dominated by the majority of stocks in downtrends.

The trend-measuring techniques covered in the price behavior chapter should be used to establish and unwind the position. If this coincides with an intermediate cycle measure sell signal, the probabilities are more likely to favor success.

Tactics. The ideal spread conditions are as small a basis as possible. This is so because the maximum profit is the strike spread less the basis. The basis in the case of our IBM example is the premium received for the short put or 16 minus 5 for a basis of 11. If the current market basis is considered attractive for the particular spread in question, the order should be entered at that price followed by the word *debit*. This is done to obtain a basis of the current market or smaller if possible. As a general guide, the profit potential of a 10-percent drop in a stock's price during four weeks should yield a profit before commissions of more than 50 percent of the basis.

Profit Profile. The maximum profit for the vertical bear spread with puts is the strike spread

FIGURE 9–4

Profit Profile (4 weeks later)

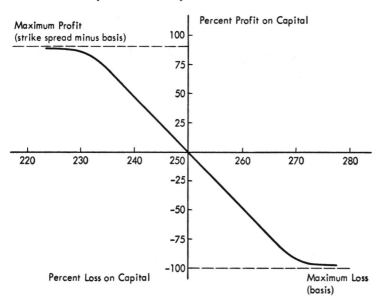

minus the basis. In our IBM exampTe, this would mean 260 — 240, or 20 less the basis of 11, or a maximum profit of $900 less commissions. The maximum possible loss is the basis or $1,100. This actually is not an ideal spread since the maximum profit is less than the maximum loss. If the numbers were reversed, the profit parameters would be favorable.

As with our other vertical spreads, whether bullish or bearish, the profit profile (see Figure 9–4) shows a rate of profit gain which is close to the rate of profit loss. This again suggests a probability of success of 50 percent, unless there is a bias in the market toward lower prices. Thus, the reliance on the market barometer to indicate a market dominated by downtrends.

A further comment should be made about these bearish spreads. For them to be successful, a significant drop in price must occur over a short period of time. This suggests good timing not only for the overall market, since it is roughly a 70-percent influence over individual stock price action, but for the particular stock in question as well. If this is so, why not simply purchase a put? The commission costs are less, the losses on trades that don't work are nearly equivalent, and with the put, the profit potential is far greater.

BUTTERFLIES

The next set of strategies are probably the most sensible of the spread potpourri in that they offer profitability over a fairly broad range of prices. These are known as butterflies, a name contributed to Wall Street jargon with the birth of tradeable options. Butterflies are a combination of a bullish vertical spread and a bearish vertical spread, where the two calls sold, in the case of a call butterfly, have the same strike prices. As the grid diagram below indicates, the two calls sold form the body of the butterfly where the long in-the-money and out-of-the-money calls form the wings.

		←——— TIME ———→			
S	*Calls*	*Near*	*Mid*	*Far*	
T	Out of the money		Buy		90
R	At the money		Sell-2		80
I	In the money		Buy		70
K					
E					

Example

Stock......................	Texas Instruments
Date.......................	June 1
Stock price................	80
Two short calls............	Oct. 80's @ 6½ each
Long out-of-the-money call...	Oct. 90 @ 1½
Long in-the-money call......	Oct. 70 @ 11

Principle. The principle of this strategy is to find a case where the sum of the call premiums of the at-the-money calls sold is greater than the sum of the premiums of the two long calls. The reason for this is that the cash flow of the spread, or the cash received less the cash spent, is positive, thereby producing a riskless hedge. This assumes, of course, that the two calls sold do not become in-the-money calls due to a rise in the underlying stock, thus threatening the spreader with exercise. The added commission costs due to exercise usually eat up the modest cash flow profit, thus producing a loss.

The maximum gain for the strategy occurs at the strike price of the two calls sold. In this case, the total premiums of $1,300 are kept, the out-of-the-money long call is a total loss and the in-the-money call purchased is worth the strike spread of ten points. Numerically, this is $1,300 minus $150 minus the small loss on the in-the-money call purchased at $1,100 (which is now worth $1,000, or a $100 loss) for a grand total of $1,300 − $250, or $1,050. The beauty of the strategy is that anywhere between a price of 70 and 90, the spread will show a profit, miniscule perhaps at either extreme.

Ideal Price Environment. The ideal price behavior for this strategy is trendless price movement. According to the market barometer's 26-year history, neutral or trendless price behavior occurs roughly one third of the time. When such dullness occurs, it usually happens after a bull market rise as stocks lose their upward momentum and begin to slowly roll over into the downtrends of the next bear market. Occasionally, such trendless behavior can occur at the end of a bear market where investors have generally lost interest. The 1949–50 period is probably the best example and it occurs very seldom.

The best guide to know when such a period has been entered is the market barometer, where neutral stocks dominate the trend composition. The best measuring technique for individual stocks is the 30-week moving average published by R. W. Mansfield Company[2] in their weekly chart service. As long as this moving average is flat, the stock is a good butterfly-spread candidate. A good monitoring technique is to place limits 5 percent above and below the extremes of the trading range the stock has swung between in its sideways trend. If these limits are exceeded, the spread should be closed out.

Tactics. The ideal conditions to search for are call premiums for an option whose strike price is close to the current stock price, where two such premiums are greater than the sum of the premiums of the long in-the-money and out-of-the-money wings of the spread. In the case of

---

[2] R. W. Mansfield and Company, 26 Journal Square, Jersey City, N.J., 07306.

our Texas Instruments butterfly, the two calls sold have a premium of $1,300, compared with the sum of the two long call premiums of $150 plus $1,100, or $1,250. The cash flow of $1,300 minus $1,250, or $50, is positive, meaning there is no loss possible in the strategy, barring commissions. Even with commission costs taken into account, the losses would be modest.

Tactically, the spreader should attempt to place the spread on at the center of the trading range defined by the sideways price trend. The easiest way to establish the position is to execute one half of the spread such as the vertical bear spread, half of the butterfly, followed by the vertical bull spread. Orders with basis limits should be used for each half in order to ensure ideal cash flow conditions.

Profit Profile. The maximum possible profit is obtained at the strike price of the two calls sold. At this price, the sold call premiums are a profit. The high-strike-price long call is a loss and the low-strike-price long call is a loss, less the gain from the low strike to the mid strike. In numbers, for our Texas Instruments case, this is a profit of $1,300 less $150 less $1,100, plus a ten-point gain from 70 to 80, or $1,300 minus $250, or $1,050. While this profit is achieved at the 80 strike price, the strategy is profitable from 70 to 90. (See profit graph in Figure 9–5.

It should be mentioned that although this strategy is designed for riskless loss conditions, early exercises of the short calls could cause enough commission costs to induce a several

FIGURE 9–5
Profit Profile (4 weeks later)

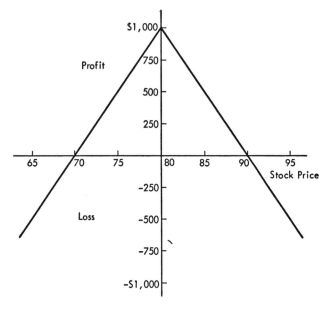

hundred dollar loss. For these reasons, the spread should use options with a minimum of three months' life. The profit of the spread should be continuously monitored so that it can be unwound if more than 50 percent of the maximum profit is obtained early in the spread's life or if the short calls are in the money in the final two weeks of the spread's life.

Butterfly spreads are possible using put options, with very much the same design as the call butterfly just described. In the put case, two puts are sold at a mid-trading range strike price, with hopes that the stock price is close to that strike. A minimum life of three months should exist for the puts. The buy side of the spread is created with the purchase of a high-strike-price put and a low-strike-price put. The key is to generate a larger cash flow on the two puts sold than is paid out for the two puts that were purchased. Again, the ideal price climate is a trendless stock in a trendless price environment.

The potential spreader should be warned that there are several disadvantages to put butterflies as opposed to call butterflies. The major disadvantage is that put premiums, except for the case of high-dividend-paying stocks, are lower than call premiums. If one has a choice, which fortunately you do, the call butterfly sister of the put butterfly should invariably offer a larger maximum gain. A second disadvantage of puts is that they are generally more susceptible to early exercise than calls, thus producing unwanted brokerage commissions. The reason for the early exercise is that the owner of a put receives cash if he exercises. If he has purchased a put to protect an underlying stock and that stock drops sharply in price, he may well prefer to decommit from the stock completely by exercising his put and selling his devastated stock to the put writer at a higher price for cash. For all these reasons, put butterflies are not recommended. The call alternative is a far more attractive strategy.

Another neutral price behavior spread has **CALENDAR** achieved a great deal of popularity and is known **SPREAD** as a calendar spread. The name comes from the attempt to make a profit from different rates of deterioration of the time premium between a near-expiring and a far-expiring call. As you may recall, the option premium graphs of Chapter 3 are nearly linear for almost the entire life of the option until the last three to six weeks. At this point, with possible exercise approaching, the commission costs of exercising begins to play an important role. The aim of the calendar spread, therefore, is to purchase a long-term call option of a given strike price and sell or write a near-term call option with the same strike price in order to capitalize on the sharper rate of deterioration of the near-term call. This same strategy can be accomplished using put options as well, which I will discuss later in this chapter. The diagram of the calendar spread with calls is as follows:

$$\longleftarrow \text{ TIME } \longrightarrow$$

S	Calls	Near	Mid	Far
T	Out of the money			
R	At the money	Sell	Buy	
I	In the money			
K				
E				

Example

Stock......................	General Motors
Date......................	May 1
Stock price...................	69
Short call....................	July 70 @ 3⅞
Long call....................	Oct. 70 @ 5¼
Basis......................	5¼ − 3⅞ = 1⅜

Ideal Price Environment. The ideal price environment for this strategy is a bit complex. If the stock remains in a narrow trading range for the life of the near-term call, the premium of the near-term short call will usually fall at a slightly greater rate than the long call. In other words the basis will widen in the favor of the calendar spreader. The real question is whether this will be greater than commission costs by a large enough margin to offer an attractive profit. What appears deceptively attractive is that, for large price moves either up or down, both sides of the spread should change by roughly the same magnitude so that the strategy appears relatively riskless. If a large rally occurs, the basis should narrow to the detriment of the spreader, while also leaving the spreader open to an early exercise of a deep in-the-money short call. If an exercise does occur, the large commission costs will usually destroy any profit potential or, worse yet, eat up most of the capital committed.

If a large price drop occurs, the basis may widen enough to offer a profit. The spread should be closed out at this point. It is tempting to only close out the profitable short call, allowing the long call to remain. This tactic runs the real risk that the decline continues, thus incurring enough of an additional loss on the long call to make the entire position a loser.

Some proponents of calendar spreads suggest that the position should be established as the underlying stock is dropping to an important trading low. At this point, the short call should be closed out and the long call held for the ensuing rally. This is an extremely high-strung approach, which relies on the ultimate in timing skills. If a trader is this capable, he would usually be better off simply purchasing an outright call option at the predicted turning point.

Gerald Appel, intrigued with calendar spreads, conducted a thorough study of the strategy, using a large sample of option quotes taken from the first several years of CBOE history.[3] Taking commissions into account, the strategy did not prove itself out. The temptation to try the strategy is great, however, because some spreads can be found with a basis of ½ or less for a high-priced stock. Since this is the minimum margin requirement for most brokerage firms, the risk seems awfully small. The major mistake is to commit a large portion of trading capital to such a venture. If the basis widens too much or early exercises occur, the losses relative to the capital committed would be devastating. If a curious spreader insists on attempting the strategy, it should be done in a price environment dominated by stocks either trendless or in downtrends. Trendless behavior is preferable.

Tactics. The object of the calendar spread is to attempt to obtain as low a basis as possible. The premium of the short call should be greater than the in-money or intrinsic value of the call. If this is not done, there is an advantage to an arbitrageur to purchase the call and exercise it, thus causing the spreader a problem.

The order should be placed at the current market basis if that is attractive with the word *debit* used after the market basis quote.

When closing out the position, both sides of the spread should be closed out simultaneously unless enough of a profit can be made on the

---

[3] Gerald Appel, *Systems and Forecasts*, Box 1227, Old Village Station, Great Neck, N.Y. 11023.

short call to provide such a low cost on the far-term long call that the spreader decides to let this low-cost call live long enough to enjoy a later rally. This case is a rare exception.

Profit Profile. The maximum possible loss of the calendar spread is the basis plus commissions incurred. The maximum possible gain cannot be determined because of the many ways the spread can be closed out. If the long call did appreciate after the short call has expired, how could the potential profit be determined?

This strategy is only recommended for traders with good timing, who are willing to mark their positions to the market daily, who commit less than 20 percent of their trading capital to their entire calendar spread portfolio.

Put calendar spreads hinted at earlier are subject to all the timing and tactics caveats of call calendar spreads. The major difference is that the strategy will work best in a neutral or rising price environment. A low basis is also most desirable because the basis in this case also represents the maximum loss plus commissions.

SUMMARY

Of all the spread strategies discussed, the butterflies are the most sensible if the ideal premium conditions can be obtained. Such opportunities are rare. All other strategies require a significant price move or good timing to produce attractive profits. In these cases, an outright purchase of a put or a call at the estimated turning point offers far more attractive risk/reward characteristics. While the lure for a sure profit strategy will keep many speculators working late hours, spreading is generally an expensive arena in which to gain an education in options.

Straddles 10

The first thing to learn about straddles is how much stock prices can move during a set period of time. This involves the study of probabilities, a word that may scare some, but it really is not that complicated. A straddle, you may remember, is the combination of a put and a call, usually with the same expiration dates and strike prices. If a straddle is purchased, the buyer is looking for either a down move or a rally of greater magnitude than the premiums paid for the two options. A writer of a straddle is anticipating that the underlying stock will move less than the amount of the premiums received, so that if an exercise occurs, the straddle writing will still be profitable. With this understood, it becomes apparent why an estimate of how large a price move is likely for the underlying stock is so important.

Both theoretical and empirical studies seem to indicate that stock prices are best described by a log-normal probability distribution.[1,2] In other

---

[1] Paul H. Cootner, ed., *The Random Character of Stock Prices* (Cambridge, Mass.: MIT Press, 1967).

[2] Gerald Appel, *Systems and Forecasts*, vol. 4, no. 14, April 14, 1977, ℅ Signalert Corporation, Box 1227, Old Village Station, Great Neck, N.Y. 11023

FIGURE 10-1

Comparison of Empirical Distribution of Stock Prices with Log-normal Distribution

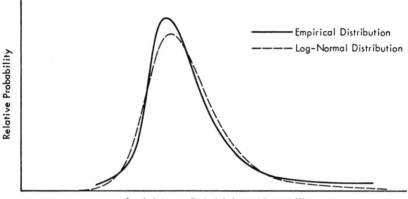

Source: Gary Gastineau, *The Stock Options Manual* (New York: McGraw-Hill, 1976)

words, the logarithms of prices have the familiar bell shaped curve used by school teachers to scale test scores.

The degree of price movement predicted by this method for a stock with average volatility rising at a rate of 5 percent per year is as follows:

3-Months Percent Change	Theoretical Chances in 100	6-Months Percent Change	Theoretical Chances in 100
+64 and higher	2	99 + higher	2
+42	5	63	5
+28	9	42	9
+16	15	24	15
+ 6	19	9	19
− 3	19	− 4	19
−12	15	−16	15
−21	9	−27	9
−28	5	−36	5
−38 + lower	2	−47 + lower	2

Suppose you want to evaluate a particular strategy for IBM. The first step is to compute the stock's volatility[3] as follows:

$$2 \times \frac{\text{(52-week high} - \text{52-week low)}}{\text{52-week high} + \text{52-week low}}$$

The average volatility is 0.53. If a particular stock's volatility is 0.65, this should be divided by 0.53 to obtain a ratio of 1.22. This ratio should be multiplied times the percent changes in the above tables to adapt them to a particular stock. For our IBM case, the volatility is 0.47 and the ratio is 0.89. With IBM at a price of 250, the workout would be as follows:

3-Months Percent Change			Stock Price	Theoretical Chances in 100
+64% × .89 =	57%		250 + 57% = 393	2
+42% × .89 =	37%		250 + 37% = 343	5
+28% × .89 =	25%		250 + 25% = 313	9
+16% × .89 =	14%		250 + 14% = 286	15
+ 6% × .89 =	5%		250 + 5% = 263	19
− 3% × .89 =	− 3%		250 − 3% = 242	19
−12% × .89 =	−10%		250 − 10% = 225	15
−21% × .89 =	−19%		250 − 19% = 202	9
−28% × .89 =	−25%		250 − 25% = 187	5
−38% × .89 =	−34%		250 − 34% = 165	2

Let us assume that we have written an IBM straddle where we have sold an IBM October 260 call at 7 and an IBM October 240 put at 5. The total premiums collected are $1,200. If the stock price closes below 228, the loss on the

---

[3] Note: This is the standard Malkiel volatility presented in the option premium chapter. We are using this measure here to be able to use Gerald Appel's probability work.

honoring of the put exercised or $1,200 (240 − 12 = 228) matches the $1,200 in premiums collected. This is the lower breakeven price for the strategy. The profit profile in Figure 10–2 graphically portrays this relationship. If the stock price is 12 points above the call exercise price of 260, or 272, the call exercise loss equals the premiums collected, thus defining the upper breakeven. Beyond these breakeven levels, each point away represents a $100 loss. Taking this all into account, we can apply our probabilities to determine whether this will be a profitable strategy if done repeatedly over time. The rest of the probability study is accomplished as follows:

Stock Price at Exercise	Profit/(Loss) at This Price	Theoretical Chances in 100	Probability-Weighted Result
393.....................	($12,100) ×	2 =	($242)
343.....................	($ 7,100) ×	5 =	($355)
313.....................	($ 4,100) ×	9 =	($369)
286.....................	($ 1,400) ×	15 =	($210)
263.....................	$ 900 ×	19 =	$171
242.....................	$ 1,200 ×	19 =	$228
225.....................	($ 300) ×	15 =	($ 45)
202.....................	($ 2,600) ×	9 =	($234)
187.....................	($ 4,100) ×	5 =	($205)
165.....................	($ 6,300) ×	2 =	($126)

Expected Loss..($ 1,387)
$\left(\begin{array}{l}\text{Sum of the Individual}\\ \quad \text{Probabilities}\end{array}\right)$

By weighting each possible result by the probability of achieving that result, a statistic called the expected outcome is obtained. In our special straddle case, the expected outcome is a loss of $1,387. This is an interesting result, because

FIGURE 10–2
Profit Profile

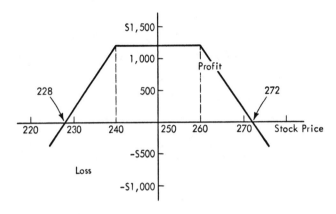

the initial reaction to a strategy offering a profit over a range of 228 to 272 is to wonder how one can lose. The probability study says that if the position is established and forgotten, the odds in the long run suggest a losing result. This is not to say that the strategy cannot be operated profitably, but a trading approach is required.

The essence of this straddle strategy is to write a straddle combination of out-of-money options. For a floor trader who can monitor small price changes and pay low commissions, the strategy offers an interesting way to capitalize on the time erosion of premiums. In a trendless and nonvolatile market, a trader can close out the put side of the position at a trading cycle high and the call at a trading cycle low. Another way to manage the position is to set predetermined price levels above and below the stock price where the position was established, as points to close out half of the straddle. Since the breakeven levels were 228 and 272, action prices of 245 to close out the put and 255 to close out the call would at least allow a profit to occur on the position as long as the stock continued to move in the same direction. The age-old problem with straddle strategies are whipsaws or large price swings back and forth across a price range. For this reason the ideal circumstances are modest price changes in a trendless market, as mentioned before. The price paid in dealing with straddles is eternal vigilance of the underlying stock price and the option premiums.

Let us eval ate a conventional straddle with IBM. In this case, we will write a conventional straddle, using an IBM October 260 put and call. The put premium in late June with the underlying stock at 258½ is $925. The call premium is $912.50 or roughly $912. The combined premiums are $1,837. As the profit profile in Figure 10–3 indicates, the strategy is profitable from a price low of 241⅝ to a price high

FIGURE 10–3
Profit Profile

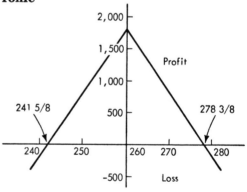

of 278⅜, commissions notwithstanding. As a rough estimate, commissions can be considered as $25 per option, per transaction, or $100 to establish and unwind the position. This would narrow the breakeven levels one point. But, back to the basic strategy. If we use our probability tables for a three-month move in IBM, the workout would be as follows:

Stock Price	*Profit/(Loss)* at this price	*Theoretical Chances* in 100	*Probability- Weighted* Result
258½ + 57% = 406......	($12,762) ×	2 =	($255)
258½ + 37% = 354......	($ 7,562) ×	5 =	($378)
258½ + 25% = 323......	($ 4,462) ×	9 =	($402)
258½ + 14% = 295......	($ 1,662) ×	15 =	($249)
258½ + 5% = 271......	$ 737 ×	19 =	$140
258½ − 3% = 251......	$ 937 ×	19 =	$178
258½ − 10% = 233......	($ 862) ×	15 =	($129)
258½ − 19% = 209......	($ 3,262) ×	9 =	($294)
258½ − 25% = 194......	($ 4,762) ×	5 =	($238)
258½ − 34% = 171......	($ 7,062) ×	2 =	($141)
Expected Loss...........			($ 1,768)

Again, we have a case where in the long run, the strategy is expected to lose money if the position is established then forgotten until expiration. To prevent losses, an investor working with such a strategy should set decision points above and below the price at which the strategy was established in order to close out the threatened side of the straddle. These points should be set close enough to the strike price of the straddle so that the loss incurred still allows a profit for the strategy. For our IBM straddle, these points could be 250 to close out the put, or 270 to close out the call. Even if this occurred in the first month of the straddle's life, the losing side of the straddle would probably have lost roughly $500, thus allowing the overall strategy to produce a profit of nearly $400. The important assumption, as usual with straddles, is that once an action point is triggered, the stock continues to move in the same direction. If a stock did reverse and trigger the opposite action point as well, enough time will probably have passed from the initiation of the straddle to allow the premiums written to lose time value and therefore further protect some of the profit. If the second action point was triggered at a later date, the strategy would probably just break even.

What if the straddle were purchased instead in the midst of a bear market? We again give a probability table, in this case one for a falling market. The general table for an average volatility stock is as follows:

Bear Market Price Movement
(six-month time period)

Percent Change	Theoretical Probability	IBM Estimated Change	
68 and higher	2	68% × .89 =	61% and higher
38	5	38% × .89 =	34%
21	9	21% × .89 =	19%
6	15	6% × .89 =	5%
− 7	19	− 7% × .89 =	− 6%
−18	19	−18% × .89 =	−16%
−28	15	−28% × .89 =	−25%
−37	9	−37% × .89 =	−33%
−45	5	−45% × .89 =	−40
−55 and lower	2	−55% × .89 =	−49% and lower

Let us assume that we purchase a six-month IBM straddle with the stock at 258½, a January 260 put premium of 11½, and a January 260 call premium of 12¾. The straddle is profitable at an expiration price above 284¼ and below 235¾, commissions excluded. The workout is as follows:

Stock Price	Profit (Loss) at this Price		Theoretical Chances in 100		Probability-Weighted Result
258½ + 61% = 416	$13,175	X	2	=	$264
258½ + 34% = 346	$ 6,175	X	5	=	$309
258½ + 19% = 308	$ 2,375	X	9	=	$214
258½ + 5% = 271	($ 1,325)	X	15	=	($199)
258½ − 6% = 243	($ 725)	X	19	=	($138)
258½ − 16% = 217	$ 1,875	X	19	=	$356
258½ − 25% = 194	$ 4,175	X	15	=	$626
258½ − 33% = 173	$ 6,275	X	9	=	$565
258½ − 40% = 155	$ 8,075	X	5	=	$404
258½ − 49% = 132	$10,375	X	2	=	$208
Expected Profit					$ 2,609

The results of the buy straddle strategy are quite favorable with an expected profit of $2,609. This is not surprising considering the sizable losses expected from the straddle writing strategies. It is interesting that the results of our studies are in complete contradiction with the predicted results of Malkiel and Quandt in their landmark simulation of option strategies.[4] However, they were using over-the-counter options as their vehicle under study. These options

[4] Burton Malkiel and Richard Quandt, *Strategies and Rational Decisions in the Securities Options Market*, Cambridge, Mass.: MIT Press, 1969).

FIGURE 10–4
Profit Profile

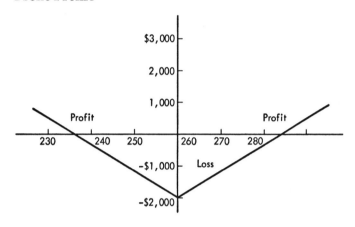

enjoyed much higher premiums and did not have an aftermarket available for nonprofitable options. In the present case, a straddle buyer or writer can close out the unprofitable side of his straddle at will. This is an important advantage.

Before ws go on to the tactics and the money management aspects of straddles, we should briefly cover the margin requirements. The case of purchasing a straddle is the simplest, since the requirements are payment in full for the option premiums plus commissions. Such a position is not allowed as equity in a brokerage account for margin purposes. For our IBM October 260 straddle, the cost is simply the sum of the two option premiums, or $1,150 plus $1,275 for a total of $2,425.

When writing straddles naked, margin requirements are computed by determining the separate coverage required for each side of the straddle, using the standard New York Stock

Exchange requirements, the necessary margin being the greater of the two individual requirements.

The three steps of the process are as follows:

1. Thirty percent of the value of the underlying stock.
2. Plus or minus a mark to the market of the difference between the current stock price and the strike price of the option under consideration.
3. Less the cash premium brought into the account as a result of writing the straddle.

For the put side of the equation, the computations for the three steps are as follows:

1. Thirty percent of the 258½ stock price is $7,755.
2. The put is 1½ points in-the-money for a debit of $150.
3. The straddle premium credit of $2,425.

Totaling the three amounts in the account form yields a total requirement of $7,265.

Debit	Credit
$7,755	
150	
$7,905	$2,425
$5,480	

The analogous computations for the call side of the straddle are:

1. Thirty percent of 258½, or $7,755.
2. A credit of $150 for the 1½ points the call is out-of-the-money.
3. A credit of $2,425 for the straddle premium collected.

The call tee account is:

Debit	Credit
$7,755	$ 150
	2,425
	$2,575
$5,180	

For our IBM straddle, the put side determines the greater margin, therefore the additional cash needed in the account is $5,480.

If 100 shares of IBM stock were owned, there would be no margin required for the call written, but the put side would require the margin for a naked put. If 100 shares of IBM stock were shorted and a straddle written, the margin required would be for the stock as well as the amount required for the naked call.

Great care should be taken by naked straddle writers to have the resources for additional margin coverage, because an initial margin requirement can change drastically if a large price move occurs and the naked option which is against the price move (i.e., a put in the case of a decline, a call in the case of a rally) demands more coverage. In short, a large price swing in either direction causes problems.

Now that we know the money requirements, what are some of the tactics of operating straddle strategies? Once again, the price environment is of utmost importance. If straddle buying is attempted, the buyer necessarily needs good price movement during the course of a straddle's life. For this reason, a cardinal rule is *avoid trading ranges in trendless stocks*. An IBM stock price chart showing more than a year of such price action is an excellent demonstration of a poor candidate for straddle buying. If our IBM October 260 straddle with total premiums of $2,475 were employed, how many price swings in the trading range have given us enough movement for a profit? Besides that, our straddle has a six-month life. A large price move should be likely well before six months is up.

Is there a measurement which could help us screen the good candidates from the chaff? An excellent guideline is the 30-week moving average plotted on the R. W. Mansfield chart shown for IBM in Figure 10–5. While this is not a pure 30-week moving average, but one whose data points are weighted from 1 to 30, the most recent data receiving the most weight, the measurement is accurate enough. On the IBM chart, as long as the 30-week moving average is flat, IBM is not a good candidate. Prior to the flat stage, or after, IBM is a good candidate.

If a stock is in an uptrend, complemented by a generally rising stock market, an excellent time to purchase a straddle is at the end of a correction which follows a several-month rise in price. The IT&T chart in Figure 10–6 offers

FIGURE 10–5

IBM Stock Price Chart

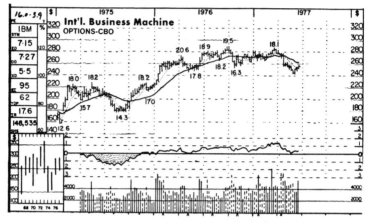

Courtesy of R. W. Mansfield and Company

several such opportunities. Notice that this stock is a candidate with a generally rising 30-week moving average. The strategy of using a straddle instead of purchasing an outright call allows for the possibility of a serious breakdown in a stock's price for which the put side of the straddle can be used to make a profit. If such a shift in price occurs, the usual practice is to close out the potentially unprofitable side of the straddle, or "lifting a leg," as it is called in Wall Street. To do this well requires some guidelines or measurements. A suggested technique is to construct two parallel lines on a chart, such as the ITT example, where the initial line is drawn across the highs of a correction in a major uptrend candidate defined by a 30-week moving average that is rising at a 10-percent, or greater, annual rate. The second line is drawn parallel

FIGURE 10–6

ITT Stock Price Chart

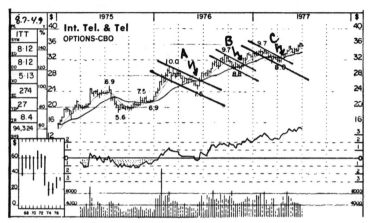

Courtesy of R. W. Mansfield and Company

to the line drawn across the reaction highs and runs through the lowest point in the reaction to date, where that low point marks a short-term reversal of a several-week down move. The point at which to establish the straddle is after three weeks of stable prices just prior to the points A, B, or C. If a downside penetration of the lower parallel line occurs, this is used as a signal to sell the call side of the straddle. The put should then be maintained until a cover short signal is obtained as outlined in the Maximum Risk chapter. If a breakout occurs on the upside of the parallel lines, this event should trigger selling the put side of the straddle. On our ITT cases, these points are marked, A, B, or C. Again, our previously discussed trendline tactics should be used to close out the call with a sell long signal.

A reverse approach can be used for downtrend

FIGURE 10–7

Eastman Kodak Stock Price Chart

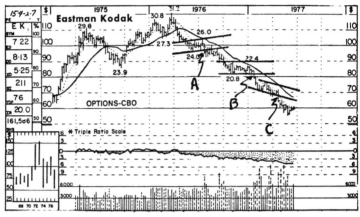

Courtesy of R. W. Mansfield and Company

candidates such as our Eastman Kodak example
(Figure 10–7). Again our 30-week moving average is the screening tool which identifies a stock
with a major downtrend dropping at a rate of
more than 10 percent annually. In this case, a
straddle can be used to establish a position
capitalizing on a hoped-for future drop in price,
while protecting oneself against a trend reversal.
For the downtrend case, the temporary pauses
are measured with a line along the lows of the
occasional rally attempts. The parallel line in
this case is drawn across the rally highs parallel
to the initial line. The straddle position is established after three weeks of prices where no new
lows are made. If the upper parallel line is penetrated on the upside, the put is closed out and
the call held until a long sell signal is given by
our Maximum Risk trend-following technique.
If the lower parallel line is penetrated on the

downside, the call side of the straddle should be closed out, with the put side held until there is a short covering signal (described in the Maximum Risk chapter). In both the examples above, the market barometer should be used to determine which version of the strategy is most likely to be profitable. If the market barometer indicates a market dominated by downtrends, the Eastman Kodak cases should be sought. In an uptrend-dominated environment, the IT&T examples should be searched for. In all cases, no more than 40 percent of trading capital should be deployed for these strategies.

Common sense might lead one to believe that the ideal environment for writing straddles is the dull, trendless environment exemplified by IBM from early 1976 through early 1977. In fact, it is tempting to think that straddles can be written naked successfully during such a period. In other words, a call and a put are written without either owning one hundred shares of the underlying stock or being short that amount. This is a trap. If a large enough price swing occurs, the straddle writer will either have to close out the losing side of the straddle or take a position in the underlying stock to cover the threatened option. Either situation means a potential profit has been missed because something has to go wrong before action is taken. Straddle writing is complicated enough without asking for trouble. Writing straddles naked is not recommended lightly.

A more realistic approach is to think of writing straddles as a variation of either fully hedged call or put writing. In a rising market environment, using our ITT example as an uptrend stock, if 100 shares of the stock were purchased at the points A, B, and C while writing a straddle, the probabilities would favor the put expiring unexercised, thus adding to the profitability of the strategy. In fact, the goal of this approach is to have the call exercised with the put and call premiums collected as profit. The ideal circumstances for the purchase-stock-write-straddle strategy is therefore to operate with the market barometer showing a market dominated by uptrends, an uptrend stock with a rising 30-week moving average, with the position established using our parallel line method for identifying the beginning of a new upsurge in the stock's price. The contrary measurement to unwind the position would be price movement below the lows which preceded the point at which the position was taken.

The short-stock–write-straddle strategy would be ideal for our Eastman Kodak example. In this case, 100 shares of stock would be sold short and a straddle written at each point that a rally attempt in a downtrend stock failed.

For our Kodak case, these are at points A, B, and C. Here the lower parallel line measuring the rally attempt offers the means of timing the position's establishment. The hoped-for result is delivery of the shorted stock against exercise of the put, while keeping the call premium as additional profit. The proper combination of circumstances for the strategy are a market barometer reading of a market dominated by

downtrends, a stock with a 30-week moving average dropping at more than a 10-percent annual
rate, with the timing of the position based on
penetration of the lower of the two lines defining
a rally attempt in a major downtrend. The contrary evidence which should cause closing of the
position is price movement back into the range
of the parallel lines.

In summary, we can say that successful straddle writing or trading depends on a measurement of the probabilities of price movement and
some timing aids for establishment or unwinding
of positions. Fundamentally oriented investors
should also seek to match the outlook for earnings growth or deterioration with the balance
of the selection criteria mentioned above.

Taxes, Margin, and Record Keeping

11

The key to consistent profits with options lies in money management, and this includes knowledge of tax laws, margin regulations, and proper record keeping.

The first aspect of taxes we will cover deals with the holder of options. A put or a call held is disposed of either through exercise of the option, sale, or expiration as a worthless item. If a call is exercised, the holder becomes the owner of the underlying stock, with the cost basis equaling the exercise price of the stock, the purchase price of the option, plus the commission costs of buying the option and exercising the option. The holding period of the call begins at the exercise date and does not include the holding period of the call. For sales in taxable years after December 31, 1976, the holding period is more than 9 months and increases to more than 12 months after December 31, 1977.

Exercise of a put by a put holder involves delivery of the underlying stock at the strike price of the option. The capital gain or loss occurs upon sale of the underlying stock. The cost of the put, the commissions for purchase of the option, as well as the commission for the sale are all deducted from the proceeds of the sale for tax purposes. These net proceeds are then compared with the cost basis of the stock to determine whether a capital gain or loss has occurred.

Taxes on puts are more complicated than taxes on calls. If a stock is held long-term prior to the acquisition of a put, the put acquired has no effect upon the holding period of the stock. If, however, the underlying stock is held short-term when the put is acquired, the holding period of the stock is eliminated and does not begin until the put is disposed either through expiration, sale or exercise. The only way to avoid this holding period elimination is to acquire the stock and the put option on the same day. The two are then considered "married" for tax purposes and should be so shown in a taxpayer's records. Then, if the put is exercised, the married stock should be used for delivery. In this case the normal holding period rules apply, but for long-term capital gains would obviously require a put with a life of more than 12 months. While such a special put could be created in the over-the-counter market, exchange traded options with such maturities are not ·available.

For the sale of a call, a capital gain or loss is incurred depending on the comparison of the proceeds with the call's cost basis. The gain is short-term or long-term depending on the holding periods stated in the first paragraph.

The sale of a put results in a capital gain or loss by comparing the sale proceeds with the put's cost basis. The holding period must be greater than 12 months after December 31, 1977. If underlying stock was held short-term at the time of the put's acquisition, any gain upon the sale of the put would always be ruled short-term. With all this complication, the simplest thing to remember is that with the new tax rules, effective after December 31, 1976, all NOCC-traded puts will only offer short-term capital gains.

If a call expires worthless, the loss is a capital loss determined by the call's cost basis. Again, after December 31, 1976, all NOCC-traded calls will result in short-term losses. As with a call, allowing a put to expire worthless results in a capital loss. If the put was "married" to the underlying stock, the cost of the put is added to the cost basis of the stock. For the purpose of handling long stock, expiration of a put closes out any short sale implications of the put.

Tax strategies for call holders used to be to make gains long-term and losses short-term. The new longer holding periods rule this out. Strategies are now more involved with the commission costs of the various alternatives. Selling a profitable out-of-the-money call does not involve this because a sale may be the only practical way to make a profit. However, an in-the-money call can be exercised with delivery taken of the underlying stock, which because of commissions will probably cost more than an outright sale of the call. It may even be cheaper to sell the call and purchase the stock separately. No matter which alternative is chosen, the holding period for the stock begins on its date of acquisition. If the anticipated sale of the call will occur prior to year-end and the holder wishes to defer the income into the following tax year, a put may be purchased to lock-in the current profit with the hedged position unwound in the following tax year.

In a loss situation where the holder also desires to defer the loss into the following taxable year, a put can be purchased or calls written to again freeze the result.

Wash sale rules apply to calls to the extent that the loss on the sale of an underlying security is deferred if a call for that stock is purchased within 30 days prior to or 30 days after the stock sale.

Put owners have usually acquired a put to protect gains either on an underlying stock or a call. But the investor must be careful because the holding period rule for puts are complicated. If an underlying stock is held short-term prior to the acquisition of a put and held until resale of the put, the holding period for the stock does not begin until after the put is sold. If more than 100 shares of stock is involved, this rule applies to the earliest acquired stock and only for the amount involved in the puts that were purchased. According to Section 1233 of the IRS Code, if the affected stock is sold after the put is acquired, the remaining stock remains untainted and the normal holding period applies.

For profitable puts, the simplest means of realizing a gain on a drop in the stock's price is to sell the put. All such gains on NOCC options are short-term. If the put holder exercises the option he may be doing so to sell stock he already owns. The gain is short- or long-term depending on when the stock was acquired. If the stock was long-term prior to purchase of the put and no other shares of the same stock were purchased in the interim, any gain or loss upon exercise is long-term. If any stock was short-term prior to purchase or was acquired after the purchase of the put, any gain on an exercise is short-term. Loss on exercise is short-term if substantially identical stock was held short-term at the time of the put's purchase.

The manner of assuring a long-term gain or loss, as already mentioned, is to acquire the put and the stock on the same day and to "marry" the two in the holder's records for the purposes of covering an exercise. The holding period until exercise then determines long- or short-term treatment. If the married put is sold at a gain, or is used to exercise other stock, the marriage is broken. Again, for NOCC puts after December 31, 1977, all gains will be short-term, unless longer than one-year option maturities are made available.

In unwinding a long stock, long put position, it is possible to realize a short-term gain on the sale of a put, holding the stock for a short-term loss at a later date. This may be especially beneficial at year-end.

For unprofitable puts, a loss may be established by either allowing the put to expire unexercised or by selling the put. For each case, based on the post-1977 holding period, all losses will be short-term for NOCC options. For a "married" put, sale of the put is necessary to establish the put's loss; otherwise, the cost of a "married" put is added to the cost basis of the underlying stock held. A strategy for achieving long-term gains is to allow the married put to expire worthless, add its cost to the basis of the stock, and continue to hold the stock for a long-term gain.

According to Revenue Code Section 1234 as amended in 1976, it is no longer possible to achieve ordinary gain or loss when entering a closing purchase transaction. For this reason, the tax treatment for writers is very similar to that for holders. The tax treatment for the premium income must await termination of the position through exercise, expiration, or by a closing purchase. Straddle writing received a ruling under the 1976 Tax Reform Act that NOCC puts and calls do not have a basis allocation problem and that the put and call are not identical. For that reason, no short sale or wash sale problems exist unless the call is exercised prior to sale of the put.

When a call writer receives an exercise notice and delivers stock to honor the obligation, this is treated as a sale. The premium is added to the exercise price and compared with the cost basis of the stock to determine the amount of gain or loss. The holding period of the stock delivered determines whether a long- or short-term gain has resulted.

The exercise of a put involves payment for and taking delivery of stock, which the writer treats as a purchase. The put premium received is subtracted from the cost basis of the stock. For holding period purposes the conservative approach is to use settlement day of the transaction rather than the earlier exercise date.

Writers of puts or calls whose options expire unexercised should treat the premium income as a short-term capital gain realized at expiration. Closing purchases for either puts or calls are short-term gains or losses as measured by the difference between the net premium received and the amount paid under a closing purchase transaction.

There are several tax strategies available to call writers. If a stock has appreciated above the strike price and an exercise notice is received, the existing long position can be sold in the open market for a greater long-term gain than would have been realized from delivery at the strike price. At the same time new stock can be purchased and delivered for a short-term loss at the strike price. This is advantageous if other short-term gains exist for offset purposes.

An alternative is to buy back the call prior to exercise, thus producing a short-term loss on the call combined with a long-term gain on the stock held. This is similar to the prior strategy except that commission costs would usually be lower, which is a decided advantage.

In a declining market, the worst of tax consequences is a likely possibility. Premiums collected from expiring calls are short-term, while losses on underlying stock held may be long-term. To avoid this problem, an option writer may wish to establish losses on his underlying stock while they are still short-term in nature. An interesting twist is to use the short sale characteristics of a put to act as a hedge, while holding stock that might otherwise be long-term in anticipation of the stock's recovery. In this case, the nature of a put, which eliminates the prior holding period of the stock, is an advantage. Such stock can only become long-term by holding it the required period after closing out the put position.

For put writing, where the writer simply sells a put, keeping cash on hand to take delivery of the underlying stock, a declining market can be a problem. If a put is written with a 100 exercise price and a premium of $800 and the stock drops by more than $800 by exercise time, the writer must take delivery of a stock by paying $100 where the current market price may be far below that. The pleasant result occurs if the market rises and the put premium for the unexercised option is kept as a short-term capital gain.

If the put is exercised, the writer has a long position in the underlying stock where the cost basis of that stock is the exercise price less the net premium received plus commission costs. The holding period for the stock begins with the exercise. If a writer, in holding his position, faces the risk of an unwanted exercise, he should close the position with a closing purchase transaction. The gain or loss with regard to the put premium is a short-term gain or loss.

Unwelcome exercise for call writers is a problem in rising markets and late in an option's life. If a call is deep in the money, occasional drops in the option premium below the in-money value of the call will entice an arbitrageur to

take advantage of the situation, and the writer
runs the real risk of exercise, possibly well before expiration time. For this reason the writer
should seriously consider closing his option
position, especially if he has the opportunity of
realizing a long-term capital gain on the underlying stock if held a while longer. An alternative
is the purchase of new stock to honor the exercise, as long as the new stock is purchased at
least 31 days after the original purchase. This
approach allows the holding period on the original stock to continue unobstructed. If the writer
did not do this and refused to immediately deliver his stock on the exercise, the stock used by
his brokerage firm to honor the exercise would
involve the writer in the sale of stock he did not
own, or a short sale. If this did occur, the original holding period on the investment stock
would be erased, and a new holding period
would begin only after newly purchased stock
was used to cover the short sale.

For more complicated strategies such as
spreading, whether with puts or calls or combinations thereof, each individual option receives
its own gain or loss. With the new tax laws these
are always short-term in nature. If the simultaneous purchase and sale of identical options is
engaged in, whether it be pairs of puts or pairs
of calls, the investor should be careful to unwind each side of the transaction on different
dates. Otherwise the IRS can view the transactions as a form of tax avoidance. One possible
problem is that a loss on a closing purchase
could be added to the cost basis of the purchased
option. This is another area where confusion in

the tax laws exist. For this reason it is wise to have a good tax consultant to call on when investing with the more complicated option strategies.

Some important changes have occurred for special types of organizations pursuant to the 1976 Tax Reform Act. Some special considerations are:

1. For regulated investment companies, elimination of the ordinary income status of premium income has opened the door to include options as an investment tool. The specifics, especially from an important Ways and Means Report regarding changes in the option tax law, say that income received on expiration or closing transactions should be treated as income from the sale or other disposition of a stock or security. This includes such option transactions in the 90 percent of the 90–10 rule.[1]

2. Personal holding companies have had an attractive investment tool taken away, namely, option premium income which fell outside of personal holding company income. With the present capital gain or loss treatment for premium income, there is no special advantage in investing with options. The capital gains from options are excluded from personal holding company income so that options do not affect its determination.

3. For tax-exempt organizations, option pre-

---

[1] Report No. 94–1192, House of Representatives, 94th Congress, 2d Session, May 26, 1976.

miums are no longer considered unrelated business income, a fact that once threatened tax-free status. However, there are many guidelines which such organizations follow and these should be checked carefully to determine the specific details from their particular supervisory authority. A further complication comes from the Pension Reform Act of 1974, which extended "prudent man" rule to trustees and fiduciaries of pension and profit-sharing trusts. Uncovered writing of puts and calls is an especially sensitive area which should be investigated thoroughly before any commitment is made.

4. For Section 1244, business corporations which cannot derive more than 50 percent of aggregate gross receipts from royalties, rents, dividends, interest, annuities, or sale or exchanges of stock or securities, option transactions now fall into that category. Care should be taken that an additional option activity does not threaten the 50-percent aggregate.

5. Subchapter S Corporations only retain their special status if they do not receive more than 20 percent of their gross receipts as passive investment income, which includes interest, dividends, and gains from sale of stock or securities. This means that option transactions are now subject to consideration as passive income.

6. For nonresident aliens and foreign corporations, the capital gain or loss nature of option transactions means that a clear

United States tax liability exists which should be withheld at the source.

7. For U.S. corporations that receive dividends from other domestic corporations, there is an 85-percent tax deduction on such dividends. While this deduction is not threatened if an NOCC put is purchased, the holding period will not accumulate during the time a put is held. Specifically, the corporation must hold the stock naked for at least 15 days prior to and after the ex-dividend date of the paying corporation.

8. Several important considerations for estate and gift tax purposes are the following:

   a. For the holder of an option, the option is valued for estate tax purposes on the properly selected valuation date.[2]

   b. There is an allowance for increase in basis limited to fair market value for federal, state, and inheritance taxes.

   c. For gift tax valuation the basis can be increased only for the federal gift tax.[3]

   d. Any gain or loss upon disposition of an option acquired from a decedent is treated as long-term capital gain or loss even if proper holding periods cannot be met.

MARGIN REGULATIONS

Margin regulations are uniform for all fungible options, whether they are the CBOE or NOCC[4] variety.

Purchased calls must be paid for in full and

---

[2] Internal Revenue Code Sections 2031 and 2032.

[3] Internal Revenue Code Section 1015 (d).

[4] National Options Clearing Corporation, the guarantor for American Stock Exchange Options.

have no loan value in a margin account. Payment must be received in one business day or the broker will take action to obtain the funds from the investor's account.

A fully hedged call writing position requires no margin on the call except that the determination of equity in the account is limited to the lower of the value at the strike prices of the calls written or the market price.

For writing uncovered calls the rules are as follows:

1. Thirty percent of the current market value of the underlying stock is required.
2. The 30-percent requirement is reduced by the amount of the call premiums collected.
3. Margin is increased or decreased by the amount the option is in or out of the money.
4. The mimimum margin is $250 per contract.

For fully hedged put writing, the margin requirement is for the short stock with additional margin required on the put itself.

The uniform margin regulations for fully hedged spread positions, in effect since February 1975 essentially require a deposit equal to the maximum loss of the spread. The rules apply *only* if the short calls expire on or before the expiration date of the long calls and require that an equity of $2,000 exists in the margin account engaged in spreading. The formula to compute this maximum loss is essentially:

Cost of the Long Calls *Minus* Premiums Collected on the Short Calls *Plus* the Loss Incurred, if any, by Purchasing the Stock

to Honor the Short Calls at the Exercise
Price of the Long Calls.

**RECORD
KEEPING**

Record keeping is the difference between a
successful and an unsuccessful money manager.
When it comes to money, the temptation is to
hide from the facts because this is where the ego
comes into play. The greatest psychological
block to overcome is the admitting of a mistake,
because for some reason the ability to make
money in the stock market is associated with
genius. Too many of us want to be a genius in
the eyes of our peers. That is our downfall.
There are two antidotes for this poison. One is
not to let anyone know what you are doing and
the other is to keep an exact record of where
your positions stand. If a problem begins to
arise, it should be corrected while it is a small
problem. In fact, it is this day-to-day correcting
which also distinguishes a successful options
money manager. The essence is to work with the
facts.

Quite obviously the records break down into
those used to design a position, those used to
monitor the position, and a summary of the results to date. Since writing naked is a rather
straightforward procedure, the design approach
will focus on hedged positions, especially partially hedged.

Figure 11–1 is an example of a general table
that can be used to design virtually any hedged
position whether fully or partially hedged. If
fully hedged only one breakeven level will have
to be determined, either a lower breakeven for a
call-writing program or an upper breakeven for

FIGURE 11-1

Establishing the Position

COLUMN WRITE →	POSITION	STOCK	OPTION	STOCK PRICE	PURCHASE COST	PROCEEDS IF EXERCISED	OPTION PREMIUM	TOTAL PREMIUMS	UPPER BREAKEVEN	LOWER BREAKEVEN
				STOCK			OPTIONS		POSITION	
	LONG	500 SHS XYZ		$75	$37,500	$40,000				
	SHORT	10 CALLS XYZ JAN 80'S					$300	$3000	91	69
	LONG	1000 SHS ABX		$28	$28,000	$30,000				
	SHORT	25 CALLS ABX JAN 30'S					$150	$3750	33 3/4	24 1/4
			TOTALS		$65,500	$70,000		$6750		

MAXIMUM PROFITS = STOCK PROFIT (LOSS) @ EXERCISE + PREMIUMS COLLECTED

= $70,000 - $65,500 + $6750 = $4500 + $6750 = $11,250

CAPITAL REQUIRED = TOTAL PURCHASE COST - PREMIUMS COLLECTED = 65,500 - 6750

= $58,750

MAXIMUM PERCENT RETURN = $\dfrac{\text{MAXIMUM PROFITS}}{\text{CAPITAL REQUIRED}}$ = $\dfrac{\$11,250}{\$58,750}$ × 100 = 19.17%

a put-writing program. The object of the table is to determine the maximum profitability of the positions as well as the breakeven level protection relative to the current price of the stock. To accomplish this, the total proceeds for delivering stock at the strike price are compared with the total purchase cost of the long stock to determine an overall profit or loss on the stock side of the picture. This should be netted against the total premiums collected to arrive at the maximum profit potential. This can be compared to the total capital required to arrive at a percent return. By following this set of procedures the investor will have defined his risks and his rewards, as well as the capital required. He can adjust these to meet his guidelines before actually establishing the portfolio. In the example given, two positions, XYZ and AZX, require $58,750 in capital without the use of minimum margin requirements. The $11,250 total profit potential between the appreciation of long stock to the strike price and the collection of premiums offers a 19.1-percent pretax return for the time period involved.

The next step is the position monitoring, and this begins with a mark to the market of each position every night. The suggested form for this purpose is probably best set up in a loose leaf binder as shown in Figure 11–2. The table is broken down into a Long section and a Short section. In the case of our partially hedged call writing portfolio the two long positions are the 500 shares of XYZ and 1,000 shares of AZX. The position price, which would be the average

FIGURE 11-2

Marking to the Market

Positions Long	Position Price	Date Nov. 7, 197–	+	–
500 Shs. XYZ	75	73		$1,000–
1,000 Shs. AZX	28	28½	$500–	
Short				
10 Calls XYZ	$300	$225	$750–	
25 Calls AZX	$150	$162.50		$312.50
			$1,250	$1,312.50

Net Loss = $1,250 –$1,312.50 = ($62.50)

price in all cases, is posted next to the date column where the closing prices are logged. In this manner the current price and position price can be compared with the difference multiplied by the number of shares and recorded in the + column if a profit or – if a loss. After all entries are made, the + and – column entries are totalled downward so that an overall profit or loss for the entire portfolio can be computed. In this case it is a net loss of $62.50. The purpose of this exercise is to highlight profit opportunities or potential loss areas so that corrective action can be taken. The overall profits, if that is the case, should always be compared with the maximum potential as calculated in Figure 11–1. If this level is reached the profits should be taken.

The vertical dashed line to the right of the position price indicates where the form can be divided in two, with the right side used in the form of an overlay. This approach avoids rewriting the entire position every day and makes use of

FIGURE 11–3
Price Follow-Up

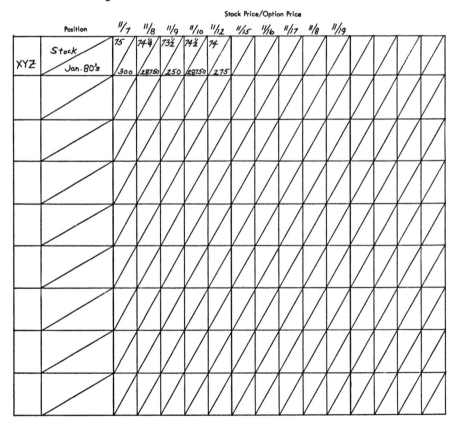

the ring binder by allowing a clean right-hand section to be laid over the previous day's results. When position changes are made a new complete page can be started.

Another important record to keep is a price follow-up as a means of learning how option premiums change with the underlying stock over time. This is a key to developing the art of money management, because one will begin to sense how the two behave together and appreciate that if enough time has elapsed, even with the underlying stock returning to the same price, the option will lose some of its premium value, perhaps a substantial amount. Figure 11–3 offers an example of such a record.

When a position becomes involved enough to have different strike price options and different expiration dates, it is imperative that a position sheet be kept as shown in Figure 11–4. This

FIGURE 11–4
Position Sheet

XYZ

OPTIONS

Buy					Sell						
Date	Opt. Shares	Strike Price	Prem.	Exp. Date	Date	Opt. Shares	Strike Price	Prem.	Exp. Date	Profit	Loss
1/31/7X	10 CALLS	80	–0–	1/31/7X	11/7/7X	10 CALLS	80	300	1/31/7X	$3,000	

STOCK

Buy				Sell					
Date	Shares	Price	Cost	Date	Shares	Price	Proceeds	Profit	Loss
11/7/7X	500	75	$37,500	1/31/7X	500	79	$39,500	$2,000	

FIGURE 11–5

Summary of Realized Gains (losses)

ACCOUNT

SECURITY	AMOUNT	DATE BOUGHT	DATE SOLD	COST	PROCEEDS
XYZ CORP.	500 SHS	11/7/7X	1/31/7X	$ 37 500-	$ 39 500-
XYZ JAN 80's	10 CALLS	1/31/7X	11/7/7X	- 0 -	3000

would be especially so for a money manager handling several portfolios, because he must keep track of which portfolio or account can be affected by a particular news event or price development. He should be able to pinpoint exactly where he has to adjust. The position sheet should accomplish this as well as providing a summary of all closed transactions, such as that involving the XYZ Corp., which yielded an overall profit of $5,000.

The final record is a statement of profits or losses which summarizes all transactions for a given year in a fashion which provides an up-to-date tax status as the year unfolds, as well as the year-end results for income tax purposes. By use of this method the usually arduous chore of unraveling a year's option activity should become simplicity itself. In the case of our XYZ Corp. transactions we have a total short-term capital gain of $5,000 (Figure 11–5).

YEAR 19___

	SHORT-TERM		LONG-TERM			
6		7	8	9	10	11
	GAIN	LOSS	GAIN	LOSS	DIVIDENDS	INTEREST
	S 20 00 –					
	30 00 –					
	S 50 00 –					

Appendix

While all evidence points to the Chicago Board type of options as the way of the future, an investor may at times desire to deal in options in non-CBOE stocks. For this reason the structure of the OTC market, how to determine option premiums, and the art of negotiating them are included in this appendix.

The traditional or over-the-counter options are contracts negotiated by a put and call broker between a buyer of an option and the guarantor of the contract, usually termed the writer. The mechanics of such a process are shown in Figure A–1. The option dealer is the core of a satellite system comprising buyers, sellers, and conversion houses. In most cases the option dealer negotiates transactions with the option department of a member firm of the New York Stock Exchange. This results from the code of business adopted in 1934, upon formation of the Put and Call Dealers Association, that all contracts are guaranteed by a NYSE member. The usual procedure is for a potential buyer of an option to ask his stock broker to purchase a call option, for example, in Xerox common stock. The usual time period is for six months and ten days so that

FIGURE A-1
The OTC Option Market

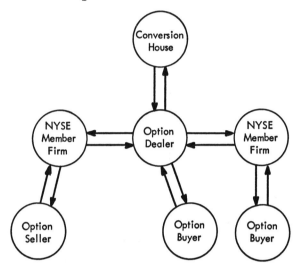

profits can be considered long term for tax purposes. The stockbroker will get in touch with
either an in-house writer of options or more
likely a put and call broker to determine whether
there are any writers interested in backing such
a contract. If the interest is found, and it should
not be difficult for such a widely held, actively
traded stock, the writer will quote a price such
as $1,450 if the stock were trading at $120 a
share. (How such a quote is arrived at will be
covered completely later in the appendix.) The
put and call broker will come back to the stockbroker through his option department with the
quote, which has been marked up slightly by the
option dealer, say to $1,500. If the customer ap-
proves, the contract will be written for that
amount at the latest market price, $120 in our
example, with the buyer charged with an addi-

tional option-writing fee of possibly $12.50 to cover the clerical work involved. The buyer is now faced with the prospect of having to make more than 15 points in Xerox during the next six months to get his money back. This is due to the $1,512.50 cost of his contract, which can only be covered if he can exercise his option, receive 100 shares of Xerox at a cost of $120 per share, and resell it for that plus $1,512.50, or $135\frac{1}{8}$ to break even. The price would actually have to be slightly more in order to cover the cost of two commissions, charged according to NYSE rules, when an option is exercised. If the stock never rose more than ten points, the option buyer could still exercise his option and at least achieve a $1,000 (less two commissions and a fee) refund on his original investment. If the stock dropped below $120 and stayed there for the entire six months and 10 days, the call would be unexercisable and the writer would pocket the $1,450 he received when the contract was written.

With this background it can be seen that the buyer's viewpoint is that Xerox will enjoy much more than a 15-point rise in price, perhaps 30 points, so that he has a chance to double his money in six months. The option writer takes the viewpoint that a 15-point rise in price is probably unlikely, no less 30 points, and besides he owns the stock, so that if it does rise that much and the call is exercised he will gladly deliver the stock, take the proceeds of $1,450 plus $12,-000 for his 100 shares at $120, buy another 100 shares and write a new option. If he is doing this with his stock he was probably thinking of selling anyway, and he has done so by making a $1,450 profit on a $12,000 investment (12 percent) in six months for a 24-percent pretax annual return. If the stock had dropped instead he would have pocketed the $1,450 premium income, still owning a stock he wants to hold long term, and write another option. In this manner an experienced option writer can earn 15 to 25 percent annual pretax return on his capital on a fairly consistent basis. While this example is a very common case, there may be many other reasons why a buyer might want to own a call option aside from outright speculation in a large price change. These were covered in the material on strategies.

The essential difference between the option buyer and the writer lies in their point of view. The buyer is willing to risk a relatively small amount of money, compared with the amount needed to own 100 shares of stock outright, for the opportunity to make a large profit during the time he owns the option. If Xerox had risen to 140 during the six-month holding period, his gross profit would have been $487.50 on $1512.50 capital, for a pretax return of 32 percent, possibly in less than six months. Although not many speculators behave in this manner (they usually hold the option for the full period), the option holder can resell his option to a dealer who will give him cash, less a small discount, for the valuable option. An alternative is to have his stockbroker exercise the option by taking delivery from the option writer of 100 shares of Xerox, paying him the $120 "strike" price of the option, and reselling the stock in the market for $140. Or, the stock purchased could be held for even higher prices.

The option writer holds the viewpoint that 20-point moves don't occur that often in a stock like Xerox, and that, rather than having to be right in forecasting such a move, he would prefer to make a more modest but consistent return on his capital. It is not necessarily that one approach is more correct than the other. It really depends on the style that is most comfortable to the individual involved. Option writing may be too dull or calculating for some, yet, to an investor seeking a relatively assured return, twice the amount of a savings account, buying an option for a large price change is a sheer gamble. The writer demands more certainty.

Who makes more money over time? That answer is not entirely clear. As Leo Pomerance will attest, any strategy adhered to rigidly for a long enough period will eventually lose an investor's capital. The answer seems to lie in adapting to the current stock market environment. For example, some accomplished traders will regularly make money buying put options in a bear market, while some writers lose a great deal of money writing calls naked (without being long the underlying stock).

Getting back to the diagram in Figure A–1 for a moment, we have not covered two elements, the option buyer who deals directly with an option dealer and the conversion house. Some active option buyers find that having an account directly with an option dealer is the most sensible way to transact their business. In most cases they don't exercise successful options, but rather sell them back to the dealer for cash. Since this is instantly credited to their account, they have the proceeds available for additional trading. Such close dealing will usually provide the trader with a lot of merchandise he might not otherwise be aware of. The house brokers, seeing the trader as an active buyer, will often show him transactions such as unexpired options just cashed in that he might want to buy for the time remaining. In addition, the paperwork of a NYSE firm having to deliver the trader's options to the dealer when cashing in, a bothersome task to some NYSE members, is avoided, along with potential accounting foul-ups by a member firm who may not emphasize option activities.

The conversion house is the banker for the over-the-counter option system, converting put options to calls or the reverse. The conversion process is necessary to counter the imbalance in the option business that is due to the phenomenon that the great majority, roughly 70 to 80 percent, of option buyers buy calls, not puts. This seems to be a parallel example of the reluctance on the part of traders in regular common stock to sell short.[1] For some reason most people approach the stock market with hope, not despair, and find it more natural to think of prospects improving, not deteriorating. This natural shortage of puts is a problem for the option

---

[1] Selling short or reverse buying is a process of selling borrowed stock immediately, it is hoped at a high price, and buying (covering short) later at a lower price to return the borrowed stock.

dealers who have many clients interested in writing straddles (a combination of a put and a call in the same stock with the same strike price and expiration date) and not enough buyers for all the puts they create. The conversion house purchases puts in exchange for calls, as well as converting calls to puts if requested. The conversion process is done risk-free and profitably. To convert a put to a call, the conversion house purchases the put, sells a call with the same strike price and expiration date and purchases 100 shares of the underlying stock. In this manner the house has protected the call obligation by fully hedging the call commitment assumed. If the stock rises in price, the gain in the 100 shares of stock is offset by the increase in the call obligation. On a fall in price, the put owned gains in value what the stock position loses. To convert a call to a put the conversion house buys the call, sells short 100 shares of the underlying stock and sells the desired put. The same principle holds of ending up with a fully hedged position, now a put obligation that is protected by a short stock position. If the stock price rises, the call owned offsets the loss in the shorted stock.

The profit made from the conversion process stems from several sources, the major one being the fee received to more than cover normal interest charges for the purchase of stock when converting a put, or the shorting of stock when converting a call. This is just compensation for the capital required in the conversion process. The conversion house also charges a nominal "floor" brokerage or paperwork fee as well as a fee for taxes incurred. If call options converted are exercised early, the house keeps the interest fee for the entire period. In addition, if the calls are exercised and the stock later drops in price, the puts held by the house become valuable and can be exercised for a profit.

NEGOTIATING PREMIUMS

Negotiating premiums is the key to a successful operation in over-the-counter options.

Naturally, a writer of options wants to receive as much as he can for the options he guarantees, while the buyer wants as low a premium as possible in order to make it easier to gain a profit on a relatively small stock price change. Contrary to some beliefs, there are no magic formulas or computerized methods used by the over-the-counter brokers to price options. A new trader usually spends six months in apprenticeship learning how to correctly quote options in many different types of securities and for different time periods. The process is essentially one of properly compensating a writer for the price volatility risk he encounters in his operation. If a premium is too small and a stock suffers a sharp drop, a call writer can suffer a large loss on the stock he holds while guaranteeing the option. With a fatter premium, his risk of such a loss is decreased.

There are six factors generally considered by a dealer in pricing an option. They are the dividend paid on the common stock (which goes to the buyer of an over-the-counter call upon exercising), the Standard & Poor rating of the stock, whether A, B, or C, the price/earnings ratio, the availability of option contracts for a given stock, the number of shares outstanding, and the fundamental outlook for the company involved.

Probably the simplest way to organize these variables is through the scoring system detailed in Table A–1. The logic is that anything which increases the writer's risk of holding 100 shares of stock to guarantee the call must be compensated for through a higher premium. If a reason-

TABLE A–1

Pricing a Six Month OTC Call
(base premium for six month call = 5%)

Factor	*Scoring*
1. Dividend..................	Add ½ of annual yield to base premium, i.e., if dividend yield = 6%, divide by 2, = 3%. Add to 5% base = 8%
2. S & P rating...............	A rating—no change in base B rating—add 3% to base C rating—add 6% to base No rating—add 8% to the base
3. P/E.....................	0–10—no change in base 11–20—add 1% to the base 21–40—add 3% to the base 41–60—add 5% to the base 61 + —add 7% to the base
4. Option availability.........	Frequently quoted—no change in base Seldom quoted—add 3% to base Have to search hard for a writer—add 6% to base
5. Shares outstanding.........	100,000 to 2 million shares—add 5% to base 2.1 million to 25 million shares—add 2% to base 26 million shares plus—no change in base

6. Fundamental outlook........	Positive—no change in base
	Negative
	   a). Disappointing earnings—add 2% to base
	   b). Serious threat to future earnings—add 5% to base

able premium is desired for a six-month ten-day call on American Telephone the stock's risk profile in Table A–1 must be checked as follows:

	AT & T Risk Profile	Score (percent)
1.	Dividend yield/2 = 6.1%/2 = 3%........................	+3
2.	S & P rating = A+.....................................	0
3.	P/E (price/prior 12 months earnings) = 10................	0
4.	Option availability = most active option written...........	0
5.	Shares outstanding = 554 million........................	0
6.	Fundamental outlook = positive.........................	0

Score = 5% base + 3% = 8.5%
Actual market quote = 7.5%
(3¾ on a stock price of 50)

The General Motors risk profile in the midst of gasoline shortages, an energy crisis, and a 30-percent drop in the sales of large cars looked like this:

	*General Motors Risk Profile**	Score (percent)
1.	Dividend yield/2 = 10.2/2 = 5%........................	+5
2.	S & P rating = A−.....................................	0
3.	P/E (price/prior 12 months' earnings) = 5................	0
4.	Option availability = frequently quoted..................	0
5.	Shares outstanding = 286 million shares..................	0
6.	Fundamental outlook = market concerned with cloudy future earnings...	+2

* Note-all these statistics are available in Standard & Poor's Security Owners Stock Guide, obtainable from any stock broker.

Score = 5% base + 5% + 2% = 12%
actual market quote = 11.1%
(5¾ on a stock price of 51⅜)

Natomas' risk profile at a time when the Indonesian government threatened to up its participation in oil company profits was as follows:

	Natomas Risk Profile	*Score (percent)*
1.	Dividend yield/2 = 0.4%/2 = 0.2% = 0	+0
2.	S & P rating = B	+3
3.	P/E (prior 12 months' earnings) = 51 3/4/.68 = 76	+7
4.	Option availability = frequently quoted	0
5.	Shares outstanding = 4 million shares	+2
6.	Fundamental outlook = market concerned with serious threat to future earnings	+5

Natomas score = 5% base + 17% = 22%
actual market quote = 12¼ on a stock
price of 51¾ = 23.7%

For Syntex, a drug stock coming back into favor after a disappointing loss of a major supply contract, the profile looked like this:

	Syntex Risk Profile	*Score (percent)*
1.	Dividend yield/2 = 0.7/2 = 0.35% = .5%	+½
2.	S & P rating = B+	+3
3.	P/E (price/prior 12 months' earnings) = 50 3/8/1.62 = 31	+3
4.	Option availability = frequently quoted	0
5.	Shares outstanding = 20 million shares	+2
6.	Fundamental outlook = market concerned with recent drop in earnings plus government investigation of drug prices	+5

Score = 5% base + 13.5% = 18.5%
actual quote = 10¾ on a stock price of 50⅜ =
21.3%, indicating an expensive option.

For four very different companies the scoring method was extremely close to the actual market quote and in two cases slightly lower than the market. This is helpful for negotiating purposes because it will prevent a buyer from paying too high a price for his options. The only subjective aspects of the scoring system are option availability and fundamental outlook. A good broker should know whether options are readily available or not, but the buyer should know that most well known blue chip stocks such as American Telephone or General Motors are very popular, as are the five or so current trading favorites. The fundamental outlook can be checked with a broker, who will say things look positive or the market is concerned about the recent government anti-trust suit, etc. If the buyer finds it difficult to agree with the severity of the current fundamental outlook, he can try to buy the option at a price reflecting his outlook or simply pay up. Armed with his scoring method he has at the least a basis for making a judgment.

What about call options with maturities other than six months and ten days, or puts? The simple rule to remember is that all call options are priced relative to the six-month ten-day time period. The rules of thumb are generally as follows:

TABLE A–2

Pricing OTC Calls for Different Time Periods

Time Period	Premium Rule
30 days	$\frac{1}{2}X-\frac{1}{20}X$
60 days	$\frac{1}{2}X$
90 days	$\frac{2}{3}X$
6 month 10 day	X
1 year	$1.5X$

Here is an example using the General Motors 6 month 10 day call option with a stock price of $51\frac{5}{8}$ and a premium of $5\frac{3}{4}$.

TABLE A-3

A Sample Pricing Exercise

Time Period	Option Premium
30 days	$\frac{1}{2}X - \frac{1}{20}X = 287.50 - 28.75 = 258.75 = 2\frac{5}{8}$
60 days	$\frac{1}{2}X = 575 \div 2 = 287.50 = 2\frac{7}{8}$
90 days	$\frac{2}{3}X = 0.67$ times $\$575 = 385.25 = 3\frac{7}{8}$
6 month 10 day	$\$575 = X$
1 year	$1.5X = 1.5$ times $\$575 = \$862.50 = 8\frac{5}{8}$

Notice that the final quotes in Table A–3 are rounded up to the nearest stock type quote in terms of eighths. The 30-day call ends up as $2\frac{5}{8}$ or 262.50 rather than 258.75, the reason for this convention being that it is easy to relate the option cost to the amount of price movement needed by the call buyer to make a profit. For the 30-day call the quote of $2\frac{5}{8}$ would tell him that he needs at least that much of a rise in the price of General Motors during the next 30 days, or $51\frac{5}{8} + 2\frac{5}{8} = 54\frac{1}{4}$ to break even on his call cost. Of course this doesn't include the two commissions he would be charged to exercise his call.

For time periods differing from the usual ones found in Table A–3, the square root rule can be applied. Again the six-month ten-day option is used as the benchmark. If a $1\frac{1}{2}$ month option were to be priced the time period of roughly 45 days would be divided by 190 days for the six-month ten-day option to obtain a ratio of 45/190 or 0.237. The square root of 0.237 is 0.487 which when multiplied times the $575 premium for the standard option yields $280 or $2\frac{7}{8}$ according to stock market quotes. As we will see later, our quoting methods are guides to assist in negotiating a fair premium, not an unbendable rule.

Puts are quoted differently and can vary much more widely than call quotes for a given stock. The reason for this is that there is usually an excess supply of puts available compared to the demand for them. As mentioned before, puts are the byproduct of writing straddles, the combination of a put and a call, which most option writers prefer because they can earn a greater return for the capital they have tied up in the 100 shares of stock guaranteeing the option. If the stock involved is a frequently written one such as American Telephone, the put premium is considered gravy by the writer and he is willing to settle for a lower than usual premium just to get the added income. In general, the roughest rule of thumb is that a put premium is 45/55 of the corresponding call premium. For our six-month ten-day General Motors call, the $575 premium would be reduced by 45/55 times $575 or $4\frac{3}{4}$ for the put. Another rule is the premium of the call minus the stock price or $575 - 51\frac{5}{8} = \$5\frac{1}{4}$ for an inactively written stock or the call premium minus two times the stock price or $575 - \$103.25 = 4\frac{3}{4}$, matching the 45/55 quote. For a put buyer it is probably simplest to use the 45/55 rule and then determine from your broker whether the put is easy or difficult to obtain. If easy you may be able to shade the premium in your favor. If not, you may have to pay slightly more than 45/55ths.

Is there a link between OTC and CBOE options? The simple answer is that the CBOE provides such an excellent market for writers and buyers to deal with each other that, whenever a new stock is added to the CBOE roster, the OTC market for that call option dies. In addition, the writers of CBOE calls obtain all dividends, in the OTC market they don't; therefore, why write OTC calls? The interesting phenomenon is that while the CBOE does not offer puts, OTC put premiums for stocks written on the CBOE generally have higher quotes than the CBOE calls. The difference is usually 10 to 15 percent of the CBOE call premium.

Which brings us back to the purpose of determining fair quotes, the ability to negotiate your premiums in the OTC market.

A typical conversation between you and your broker might go something like this:

You: Hi, Jim. George here. What are you quoting six-month calls on Natomas?

Your broker: Let me check. (pause) I think I can get several for you at $12\frac{1}{2}$; the current stock price is $51\frac{3}{4}$. How many do you want?

You: Probably no more than five. But isn't that a little high? Let me see, at $51\frac{3}{4}$ my calculations come up with about $10\frac{3}{8}$ (using the scoring method and a moderately negative fundamental outlook).

Your broker: Never!

You: Why?

Your broker: Haven't you heard about the Indonesian government threatening to change their tax rules? They want a much bigger participation. Just like the Arabs.

You: No kidding (rechecking your fundamental factor and raising it to 5%). What if I buy ten?

Your broker: Let me see what I can do. Hold on. (pause) OK. I found a writer of ten who will take 12¼ for all ten.

You: That still sounds high (your own score now says 12¼ is fair, but for a larger quantity you want somewhat of a break). I'll pay 12 flat. Take it or leave it!

Your broker: Just a second. (pause) OK. He'll do it for 12. But only if you do all ten.

You: Done.

Your broker: OK, it's yours. Ten six-month calls at 12. Let me see what Natomas is trading at now. OK, 51⅞. That's your strike.

You: OK, George.

Your broker: Do you want me to call you if I find any more?

You: No thanks. That should hold me for now. Thanks a lot, George. I'll talk to you later.

Your broker: So long.

The reader might ask, "Why do I have to know anything about the over-the-counter market if the Chicago Board Options Exchange is so popular?" The answer is that there are still many uses for the over-the-counter market, the main one being that Chicago Board options were only traded for 32 major blue chip companies as of June 1, 1974. If a holder of stocks outside this list wants to write calls or a speculator wants to capitalize on a stock price change in an issue

away from the CBOE he has to trade in OTC
options. However, as the record to date indicates,
the many superior features of CBOE options
have drawn a great deal of activity away from
the over-the-counter market.

Index